Fishing Tips
for Freshwater

Gene Kugach

STACKPOLE
BOOKS

0 11557 02654 2

Published by
STACKPOLE BOOKS
5067 Ritter Road
Mechanicsburg, PA 17055
www.stackpolebooks.com

Printed in the United States of America

10 9 8 7 6 5 4 3 2 1

First edition

Library of Congress Cataloging-in-Publication Data

Kugach, Gene.
   Fishing tips for freshwater / Gene Kugach.—1st ed.
   p. cm.
    ISBN 0-8117-2654-1 (alk. paper)
    1. Fishing—Miscellanea. 2. Freshwater fishes—Miscellanea. I. Title.

SH441 .K843 2003
799.1'1–dc21   2002030488

Dedicated to my daughter, Michelle,
and my grandchildren,
Lauren Ann and Kristen Ashley

CONTENTS

CONTENTS

CONTENTS

PREFACE

Many of the tips contained in this book have been around in one form or another for many years and have proven to be very useful to a number of fishermen.

I hope my efforts in collecting the tips presented here and compiling them into various categories help the reader to be more successful in his or her fishing endeavors.

Gene Kugach

Acknowledgments

I hesitate to mention all the sources that contributed to the making of this book. However, the following are major sources for most of the information:

Magazines:
MidWest Outdoors, Outdoor Notebook, The In-Fisherman, Bassmaster, B.A.S.S. Pros, Fishing Facts, Sports Afield, Field & Stream, Great Lakes Fisherman, Salmon/Trout/Steelheader, Fly Fisherman, Rod and Reel, Fishing World, and *Fins and Feathers*

Manufacturers' Catalogs:
Shakespeare, Eagle Claw, Mustad, South Bend, Orvis, Tackle-Craft, Trilene, Cortland, Grizzly Inc., Mister Twister, Northland Tackle Co., Lindy-Little Joe Inc., and DuPont Stren

Chapter 1

General  Fishing Tips

This chapter contains general tips on freshwater fishing. The tips cover some of the basics to help make your fishing more enjoyable.

TIP 1

Variety

Most lakes are best known for one specific species of fish (bass lake or walleye lake). River or stream fishing, on the other hand, is different and always full of surprises. Whether you're fishing from shore or from a boat, you never know what will come along and take your offering.

To be sucessful, try different presentations (lures and jigs) and a variety of baits (worms, leeches, grubs, etc.).

TIP 2

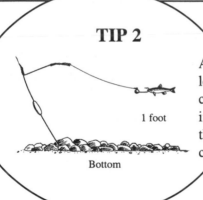

1 foot

Bottom

Fundamental Rule

A great number of fishermen have never learned the fundamental rule of river, creek, or stream fishing: Keep your bait in the fish zone, which is never more than a foot off the bottom of the river, creek, or stream.

TIP 3

Don't Spook the Fish

When stream or creek fishing, do not make a lot of noise while wading or stomping along the bank.

Most fish see and feel approaching fishermen. Sneak up on your quarry as quietly and inconspicuously as possible. Walk slowly and softly, and wear clothing that blends in with the surroundings.

TIP 4

Foam Patches

Foam

Don't overlook those foamy patches of water when stream or river fishing. Cast your lure or baited hook into the foamy areas because crippled minnows, insects, and other foods often wash into them and attract feeding game fish.

TIP 5

Minimizing Hang-Ups

To minimize hang-ups, use a lighter line (less than 8 test) and light or fine-wire Aberdeen hooks with a dropper rig for the weights.

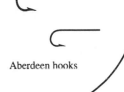

Aberdeen hooks

TIP 6

Dropper Rig

To minimize losing hooks or lures when river or stream fishing, try a dropper rig. The rig consists of a short piece of lighter test line tied to your fishing line about a foot or two above your presentation with enough split shot added to keep the offering near the bottom of the river or stream.

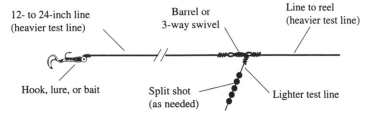

12- to 24-inch line
(heavier test line)

Barrel or
3-way swivel

Line to reel
(heavier test line)

Hook, lure, or bait

Split shot
(as needed)

Lighter test line

TIP 7

Perch Pier Fishing

The following is a list of basic equipment that can be used for shore or pier fishing for perch in the Great Lakes region.

- Two ultralight rods and reels.
- Reels filled to capacity with 4-pound test line.
- Minnow bucket with at least 4 dozen small perch minnows.
- Two dozen crayfish (crabs).
- Landing net with a 10-foot handle.
- Two dozen 10 short-shank hooks.
- Two dozen B-B split-shot sinkers (assorted sizes).
- Stringer with a 20-foot cord.
- 5-gallon carry-all pail or bucket.
- Fishing license.
- Small box for extra tackle (hooks, line, sinkers, and so forth).
- Extra warm clothing (just in case the weather changes).

TIP 8

Salmon and Trout Pier Fishing

The following is a list of basic equipment that can be used for shore or pier fishing for trout or salmon in the Great Lakes region.

- Three heavy-duty rods and reels (two to use, one as a spare).
- Reels filled to capacity (300 yards) of 12- to 15-pound test line.
- Assorted lures: silver/blue/green 3 ounces to $1\frac{1}{2}$ ounces and 2 ounces to $\frac{3}{4}$ ounce, Mr.Champs, Cleo's, assorted jigs, large streamer flies, and so forth.
- Assorted snap swivels.
- Two dozen assorted size sinkers: split shot, egg, dipsey.
- Two dozen 2/0, long-shank hooks or floating jig heads.
- Minnow bucket.
- Stringer with a 20-foot cord.
- Assorted bait: alewives, large minnows, spawn sacks, pork rind, marshmallows, whole-kernel canned corn.
- Landing net with extendable handle (10 feet or more).
- 5-gallon carryall pail or bucket.
- Fishing license with a trout/salmon stamp.
- Tackle box for extra equipment.
- Extra warm clothing (just in case the weather changes).

TIP 9

Bait Selection

Take several different types of live bait with you. A good selection will increase your chances for success.

TIP 10

Lure Sizes

Use larger, bulkier baits or lures. You'll catch bigger fish with bigger baits or lures when the fish are active.

TIP 11

Flexibility

Be mobile. Don't hesitate to try different lakes, ponds, streams, or rivers if the fish are shut off on the waters you're fishing.

TIP 12

Line

Change your line. Late summer and fall are big fish time, and you don't want to lose a trophy fish because of a bad line.

TIP 13
Fish Control

The following are a few things to remember when you hook a fish.

1. Pay attention to what the fish is doing.
2. Adjust your drag if necessary.
3. Keep a taut line.
4. If it's headed for a snag, give it some slack.
5. If it jumps, give it slack and lower the rod tip.
6. If it stops in heavy weeds, be patient, keep a tight line, and wait until it starts to move again.

TIP 14 — Boating Your Catch

The following are a few things to remember when boating your catch.

1. Never try horsing in your catch.
2. Play the fish until you tire it out.
3. Never reel in your catch up to the rod tip.
4. Allow enough line (about a rod length) to control the fish when it's near the boat.
5. Have your net ready.

TIP 15

Netting Your Catch

When netting a fish, submerge the net under the water and lead the fish into the net after it has been played out. Never scoop at the fish with the net. Most fishermen are too anxious to land their catch and don't play the fish enough to tire it out. When the fish sees the net, it dives under it, often causing the fisherman to lose his or her catch.

TIP 16

Hook
digorger

Removing Hooks

Most hooks can be removed from a fish by holding it belly up (upside down) and working out the hook. However, if the hook is deep inside the fish's mouth, use a hook digorger or cut the line.

TIP 17

Measure Your Catch

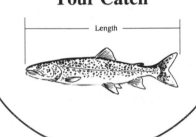

Length

It's a good idea to carry some type of measuring device with you when you're fishing. It could be a ruler, a tape, or a piece of equipment like a rod or net handle with incremental markings on it. You never know when a game warden will be around to check if your catch is legal.

TIP 18

Live Baskets

A neat way to keep your catch alive and fresh, or if you want to release it after you show it off, is to use a live basket rather than a stringer.

Live baskets come in various sizes and are made of wire mesh. They can be hung overboard from a boat or put in the water when shore fishing.

TIP 19

Hang-Ups

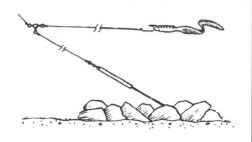

To prevent hang-ups when drift fishing over rocky bottoms, rig your line with a pencil type sinker at the end and tie in the hooks at 6- to 8-inch intervals above the sinker.

TIP 20

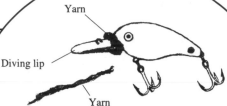

Yarn

Diving lip

Yarn

Using Crankbaits

When fishing with a crankbait, wrap a few strands of yarn around the diving lip and treat it with some liquid scent. The yarn will have no adverse effect on the lure's action, and the scent will work as an attractor.

TIP 21
Cane Polin'

Cane pole fishing is an old-fashioned, all-purpose method used to catch fish in heavy weed cover. In most cases, you use a 16-foot cane or fiberglass pole with a short line off the tip to maintain control of the lure or bait. You should work the lure or bait into the weedy pockets found in weedbeds, lily pads, or tough-to-reach areas.

Use jigs, lures, spinners, or live baits to dip gently into a pocket and then work it, using either a swimming action or the conventional up-and-down technique. Cane polin' may not be a glamorous way to fish, but it can't be beat for heavy weed cover.

TIP 22

Selecting a Lake

When spring arrives, try smaller lakes for the best fishing. Small lakes warm up more quickly than large bodies of water, resulting in more action.

A rise in water temperature of five or ten degrees can trigger some great fishing.

TIP 23

Spring Fishing in Small Ponds

In the spring, concentrate your efforts on small ponds. They warm more quickly than larger bodies of water.

Water temperature controls the spawning cycle of all freshwater fish. Small ponds will be active earlier with spawning fish.

TIP 24

Aquatic Plants

In early spring, emerging aquatic plants are great fishing areas to try. They attract baitfish, which in turn attract predators.

Cabbage plants in particular sprout up after a few warm days and are great locations for finding bass. If you find some cabbage plants, don't pass them up.

Cabbage

TIP 26
Spring Bow Fishing

When bow fishing in the spring for rough fish, remember that solid glass arrows are stronger than wood arrows. The glass arrows weigh more and make it easier to hit the mark when they are shot through 15 or 20 feet of water.

TIP 25
Green Weeds

When you start fishing in the spring, keep an eye out for green vegetation. No matter how cold the winter was, a lot of weeds survive and come up again in the early spring. These early patches of green vegetation attract early movements of bass, pike, muskie, walleye, and many species of panfish.

TIP 27
Spring Fishing

Spring is one of the best seasons for fishing. Most species spawn during the spring and are often found in the shallows. Try fishing water six feet deep or less, using small bucktails, spinnerbaits, minnows, or various types of live bait.

TIP 28

Best Spring Month

The most productive month in the spring season in all probability is the month of May. Longer and warmer days heat up the water temperatures to a point where the weed growth blossoms and the spawning season for most fish species starts.

Bass and panfish are on the beds close to shore and are easy to spot. During this period, as mentioned above, live bait and artificial lures work well.

TIP 29
Summer Fishing

Fish are harder to catch during the summer months, when live food and cover are more abundant. The fish become very selective when they feed, and gorge themselves when they do.

TIP 30
Summer Sunstroke

To keep a cool head on those hot summer days while on the water, soak a cloth or a bandanna in the water and place it inside your hat. Always wear a hat to avoid or lessen the chance of sunstroke.

TIP 31
Seasonal Changes

The great locations you found to fish in the shallows in the spring may prove disappointing when you return there in the summer and fall.

Fish seek different surroundings at different times. The fish that sought the shallows in the spring when they were spawning will move to deeper, cooler water in the summer. In the fall, most fish also seek deeper water as winter approaches.

To be a successful fisherman, you need to seek out different locations to fish depending on the season.

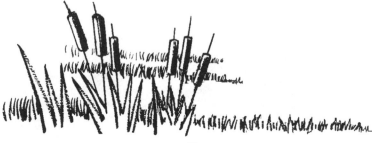

TIP 32

Fall Fishing— Rivers, Streams, and Creeks

An advantage of river, stream, or creek fishing in the fall is that you can always find an uncrowded area to fish. If it's crowded near a dam or spillway or along the shoreline, a short walk or boat ride down- or up-stream most likely will eliminate the crowd.

TIP 33

Fall Weather Changes

When the weather changes in the fall, so do fishing conditions. Fish often move to different locations and prefer different presentations when a significant change in the weather occurs.

Take a lesson from the fish, and be prepared to make some of your own changes, such as the lures or bait you use or your location.

TIP 34

Fall Season Tips

Improve your chances of a good fishing experience in the fall months with the following tips:

1. Go with larger, bulkier lures or bait.

2. Take and try several different forms of live bait.

3. Try different lakes, ponds, rivers, and streams.

4. Change your line.

TIP 35

Bugs

To avoid getting bit by mosquitos and other insects, don't use scented personal-care products or perfumes. Some insects are attracted by the smell of these products. Also remember that bugs love the early morning and early evening hours when it's cool, windless, and damp. Under these conditions, use a good insect repellent.

TIP 36

Belly Boats

In many small ponds and lakes, boats or launching facilities may not be available, thus preventing you from getting to the most productive areas to fish. To solve the problem, consider getting a "Belly Boat," an inflatable tube designed for fishing that is light to carry, easy to maneuver, and safe under most conditions.

TIP 37

Trophy Fishing

If you catch a trophy-size lunker, try the same spot on your next fishing trip.

In most species, the trophy-size fish can be found in the best spot in the lake or stream. If it gets caught, the next largest fish will move into the same spot.

TIP 38
Finding Fishable Waters Close to Home

Try using county highway maps, state maps, and topographical maps to find fishable waters near your home.

Concentrate on rivers and streams with public access areas, such as bridges, nature areas, or public parks. Also look for ponds, lagoons, and lakes that you had not known were close to your home.

After you make a few selections, do some scouting by visiting the locations and doing a little fishing. If the areas are private, don't forget to ask permission from the owner before fishing.

TIP 39
Keeping Notes

Purchase a small pocket dictating machine to make notes on your fishing trips. Record the water and weather conditions, lures or bait used, what you caught, and other information that you may want to reference later.

TIP 40
Plan Ahead

Before you hit the water fishing, have a plan.

Whether fishing from a boat or the shore, take a few minutes to study the body of water and decide on the best approach to fishing it.

Select the locations you plan to fish, prepare the equipment you want to use, and decide what type of bait or lures you want to try.

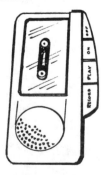

TIP 41
Fishing New Waters

When fishing a lake or stream for the first time, keep an eye out for situations that may indicate productive locations to fish. For example, if you see a fast-moving boat stop and the occupants cast or drift fish in an area, or if you see several boats anchored close to one another in a specific area, or if you see people fishing along reeds, weedbeds, or lily pads in a specific location, try those locations later.

TIP 42   Rainy Day Fishing

Don't let a rainy day keep you from fishing. Wind and raindrops knock insects into the water, attracting fish to the surface to feed and making it easier to catch them. Rain also breaks up a smooth water surface, making it harder for the fish to see the fisherman.

TIP 43
Water Level

A hot, dry summer drops the water level of a lake, exposing it's bottom along the shoreline and helping new vegetation to grow when the water rises again. The new growth provides both food and cover for the lake's fish and aquatic life.

15

TIP 45

Suntan Lotion

If you forgot to bring along suntan lotion on your fishing trip, try using vinegar as a substitute. It really works in preventing sunburn.

White Vinegar

TIP 44

Watch the Birdie

When a weather front moves through and the barometer is falling, birds tend to sit rather than fly. If you spot a bunch of blackbirds sitting still on a utility wire, you can be pretty sure that the barometer is falling and the weather will be changing.

TIP 46

Shady Structure

When fishing, don't overlook shady areas by bridges, docks, or overhanging trees. During the heat of the day, bluegills and other panfish will seek out these areas for cover from the sun. Shade is a form of structure that attracts fish. Also try deep-water openings around weed beds, lily pads, sunken stumps, or piles of debris.

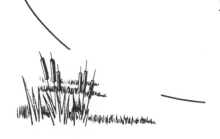

TIP 47

Five-Gallon Bucket

Take along an empty 5-gallon bucket on your next fishing trip. It may come in handy on your boat as a trash or litter container, to hold fish or bait, or to bail out the boat. If you're a shore fisherman, you can use the bucket to carry your equipment, to sit on, or to hold trash.

TIP 48

Bobber Sizes

When using a bobber, pick one that will be just big enough to support what's under it.

Most novice fishermen use a bobber that is too large. What you want is just enough buoyancy so that the fish won't detect any resistance. The right bobber will help you catch more fish.

TIP 49

BAKING SODA

Baking Soda

Every fisherman should plan to take along baking soda on his or her next fishing trip.

Baking soda can be used dry as a scouring agent to brighten dull or rusty lures.

Prevent rusty hooks by anchoring them to a cork and placing them in a bottle of dry soda.

Mix baking soda with water and use it to rid your hands, your bait bucket, or creel of fishy odors.

Make it into a paste with water, and use it to alleviate the sting of sunburn or bug bites.

Baking soda can also be used to settle your stomach after you lose the big one.

TIP 50

Good Fisherman

Fishing is a skill that must be learned. Good fishermen stay good because they fish as much as possible and they keep up-to-date in their knowledge.

TIP 51

Ask Questions

When talking to a successful fisherman, always ask at what depth the fish were taken.

TIP 52

Test the Water

When fishing unfamiliar water such as a river or stream, tie a bell sinker to the end of your line without any hooks and do some fan casting. When you retrieve the sinker, you can locate the areas to avoid such as snags, sunken logs, and so forth.

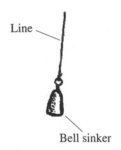

Line

Bell sinker

TIP 53

Help!

If you fish alone, take along a cellular phone. It may save your life if you're out on the water and an emergency occurs. Keep it in a waterproof container or a zippered bag on your person or in the boat.

Dial 911, if you need help.

TIP 54
Take a Kid Fishing

It's never to early to start a youngster fishing. However, it takes patience to mold one into a real fisherman. Here are some suggestions for getting a child started in fishing.

1. Pick a location where they will catch fish. The size of the fish is not important.
2. Make the youngster feel important, by helping to set up the equipment. Use simple tackle and methods.
3. Let them do their own thing. Don't bark orders, and don't give them unsolicited advice. Encourage them to ask the questions, and don't get upset if they make mistakes.
4. Make a big deal about what they catch.
5. Take a break once in a while and praise them for their efforts. Talk to them about things they like. Try to instill a deep respect for nature.
6. Quit fishing when they lose interest or they start to tire.

TIP 55
Boat Fishing

When fishing in a boat, always wear a life vest, life belt, or life preserver.
Make sure everyone in the boat wears one as well.

TIP 56
Extra Eyes

Take along or keep a pair of cheap reading glasses in your tackle box to help you thread a hook, tie knots, and untangle lines.

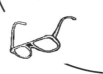

TIP 57
Catch-and-Release

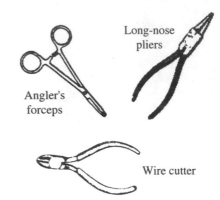

Long-nose pliers

Angler's forceps

Wire cutter

Carry a pair of "angler's forceps," long-nose pliers, or a wire cutter as part of your fishing gear. When you catch a deeply hooked fish you want to release, use the forceps or the pliers to remove the hook. Use the wire cutters to snip the hook or the line as close to the hook eye as possible.

Strong acids in the fish's mouth and stomach will eat away the hook without killing the fish. You can also use the pliers to press the barb back against the hook shank, making the hook virtually barbless.

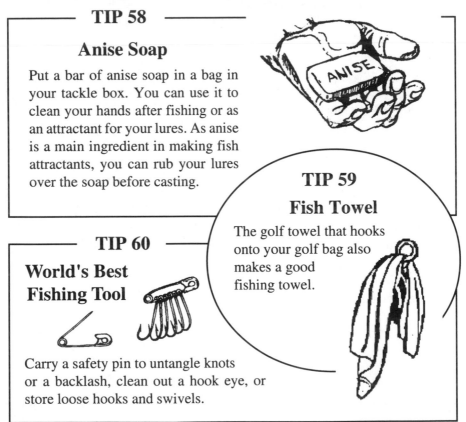

TIP 58
Anise Soap

Put a bar of anise soap in a bag in your tackle box. You can use it to clean your hands after fishing or as an attractant for your lures. As anise is a main ingredient in making fish attractants, you can rub your lures over the soap before casting.

TIP 59
Fish Towel

The golf towel that hooks onto your golf bag also makes a good fishing towel.

TIP 60
World's Best Fishing Tool

Carry a safety pin to untangle knots or a backlash, clean out a hook eye, or store loose hooks and swivels.

Chapter 2

Locating Fish

This chapter contains information on how to locate fish, with tips ranging from keeping records on locations to methods of attracting fish.

TIP 1

Structure

Catching fish means being in the right spot at the right time. In most rivers, streams, and lakes, approximately 90 percent of the water is void of fish. The secret to successful fishing is to find the remaining 10 percent of the water that has fish.

For the most part, those areas are what's known as structure—points, drop-offs, rock piles, sunken islands, gravel bars, weed beds, stumps, logs, or anything that involves a change in depth or a change in the bottom terrain. Structure areas hold the majority of catchable fish, so fish there until you locate the fish.

TIP 2

Homework

Before fishing a lake, stream, or river, do your homework. Learn as much as you can about the body of water you intend to fish. Get a map, if possible, or make your own rough map.

Talk to resort owners, bait shop owners, local residents, guides, or other fisherman. Make note of the locations they give you, the types of fish that have been caught, and any other information you may need.

TIP 3

Keeping Records

One way to mark "hot spots" is to make a map of the lake, stream, or river you're fishing and note the good locations where you caught fish.

Record the types of fish that have been caught, what bait you used, and any other information you may want to know for future trips.

TIP 4

Basic Rules to Remember When Trying to Locate Fish

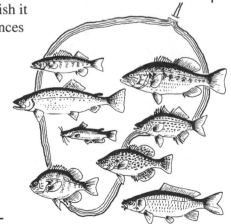

- Ninety percent of all waters contain no fish.
- Fish are creatures of habit; once you learn their habits, you can find fish.
- Fish require some form of cover (structure) in which to live (home).
- Fish require some form of cover (structure) in which to move about (migration routes) when they search for food.
- Fish concentrate in given areas where cover (structure) is available.
- Most game fish are in deep water (home) greater than 8 or 10 feet deep most of the time.

TIP 5

Structure Fishing
The Answer to Successful Fishing

Structure fishing refers to the bottom contour of a body of water, whether it is a pond, lake, stream, or river. Structure can be defined as anything unusual on the bottom of a body of water that will attract fish. Most waters that are void of structure are also void of fish.

If you can identify structure and fish it properly, you will improve your chances of catching more fish.

Basic Rules for Success

- Always fish structure.

- Learn to read structure.

- Fish where the fish live.

TIP 6

Selecting the Right Waters

Selecting which pond, lake, river, or stream to fish can be a determining factor in how successful or unsuccessful your fishing will be.

Before making your selection, ask yourself the following questions.

- What season is it?
- What are the weather conditions (cold fronts, rainy season, drought)?
- How familiar am I with the waters I plan to fish?
- How much time do I have to fish?
- What facilities are available (boat rentals, bait shops)?
- Can I get a contour map of the lake or the waters I'm planning to fish?

- What are the water conditions (polluted, clean, clear, dirty, murky)?
- How deep are the waters I'll be fishing, and is any structure available?
- What time of day will I be fishing (morning, midday, evening)?

After answering the above questions, apply the three basic rules and start fishing.

TIP 7
Water Temperature

In general, water temperature is one of the important factors in successful fishing. It governs fish activities such as feeding movements and spawning cycles. Knowing what temperature each species prefers and fishing in those waters can make the difference between a successful catch and getting skunked.

TIP 8

Mixed Bag

Don't get hung up on trying to catch a certain species of fish. Instead, concentrate on finding good fishing spots and use all-around lures and a variety of bait to be successful. You may catch lots of different species of fish, including the one you were after.

TIP 9

Local
Forest Preserves

Many states with large urban communities have established forest preserves. These parcels of land are set aside as recreational areas for public use, and many of them have lakes, ponds, rivers, or streams that are frequently stocked with fish. If you can, check them out, as they provide some excellent fishing.

TIP 10

State and
National Parks

Every state has a national or state park that provides a recreational area for the public. Many of these areas have ponds, lakes, streams, and rivers that are accessible for fishing.

TIP 11

Reservoirs or Impoundments

Many states have created reservoirs or impoundments to prevent flooding. Most are creek-, stream-, or river-fed; vary in size, shape, and depth; and include most often game fish species. They provide excellent fishing opportunities.

TIP 12

Lakes

Lakes vary in size, shape, and depth and, depending on their location within the country, include most game fish species.

They provide excellent fishing opportunities, and most of them can be fished from shore or from a boat, using a variety of equipment such as spinning gear, cane poles, bait casting gear, or a fly-fishing outfit.

TIP 13
Farm Ponds

Farm ponds, like lakes, vary in size, depth, and fish population. They can provide excellent fishing during most seasons, especially in the spring.

They can be fished from shore or a boat. Most ponds are privately owned and stocked by the owner. You need the owner's permission to fish them, and in most cases permission will be granted for a small fee.

TIP 14

Park Lagoons

Many communities have parks with lagoons that are frequently stocked with various fish species. These lagoons provide children an opportunity to experience the fun of fishing. If you have kids and a local lagoon nearby, take the kids fishing.

TIP 15
Spring Creeks

Spring-fed creeks provide some of the best trout fishing in many states. If you have a few nearby, give them a try.

TIP 16
Rivers and Streams

Rivers and streams throughout the country provide excellent fishing opportunities. They have a wide variety of catchable fish species, from rough fish to game fish. They can be fished by boat or from the shore, using most types of fishing equipment.

When fishing rivers or streams, consider the current and the structure that affects it. Most fish-holding areas will be locations where fast-moving water passes some form of structure that slows down the water and also provides cover for the fish.

TIP 17

Strip Mine or Quarry

Strip mines and quarries containing lakes with good fish populations are excellent areas to try fishing. Their lake bottoms are made up of sand, shale, slate, or gravel, which keep the water clear. Because of the water clarity, be sure to wear polaroid sunglasses when fishing to spot cruising fish or potential structure.

TIP 18

Lake Springs

When fish are fussy during warm weather, that's the time to find a deep spring hole near a shallow flat.

Once you have found the spring, offer the fish several small worms on a hook. Keep the bait a few inches off the bottom, and jig it gently every few minutes.

TIP 19

Fish Cribs

Many states build havens for fish in public waters maintained by the state. These havens are called fish cribs and consist of artificial structures made with cement blocks, hay bales, stake beds, clay tiles, brush piles, and old Christmas trees weighted with an old tire.

They serve as cover and attract fish in lake areas that are void of natural structure. Fish cribs are excellent areas to try fishing and support a variety of fish species.

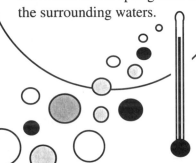

TIP 20

Locating a Lake Spring

If you're fishing a spring-fed lake and trying to locate the spring, try using a thermometer. The water temperature will be a lot cooler at the spring than at the surrounding waters.

Christmas tree

Old tire

TIP 21

Locators and Depth Finders

If you're a serious fisherman, get yourself a fish locator or a depth finder. These devices not only provide water depths, but with experience, they help you to identify weeds, baitfish, bottom structure, and game fish.

You can make yourself some great fishing maps using these devices.

TIP 22

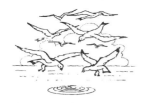

Bird Watching

While fishing, keep an eye out for diving or circling seagulls, terns, or loons. Most likely, they are feeding on baitfish schools, and wherever there are baitfish, larger game fish are nearby.

TIP 23

Mobility

Most fish are constantly on the move looking for food. They only stay a short time in one specific area to feed on baitfish or wait for a food source to come within their grasp. One secret to catching fish is mobility. Seek out the fish by trying different locations until you find a spot where the fish are active.

As a rule, don't spend a lot of time in one given location. If the fish aren't biting, move to a new spot.

Moving around a pond, lake, river, or stream is important in making consistent catches.

TIP 24
Scents

Using scents on lures and baits has become a common practice among many fishermen as well as some lure manufacturers.

Scents can be purchased in spray cans or squeeze bottles or as prepared bait in a variety of odors. They work as attractors to stimulate fish to bite.

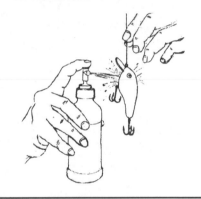

TIP 25
Chumming

Chumming attracts fish and entices them to start feeding. It can also be used to create locations where fish will congregate to feed. Do this by placing chum repeatedly in a specific area at a specific time.

One chumming method is to fill a mesh bag with cut or crushed bait and tie it with a rope to a tree. Then toss it out at a choice location, and wait a few days to fish the spot using the same type of bait.

TIP 26
Perch Chum

Here's a chumming tip to try when you go perch fishing. Make a mixture of chum using chopped fish and egg shells, and take it along on your fishing trip. When schooling perch won't touch your offering, scatter the mixture around your fishing spot to spark their interest.

The following tips cover some of the various forms of structure found in most ponds, lakes, reservoirs, rivers, and streams.

TIP 27

Points

Points are projections of land that extend out from the shore from shallow to deep water.

Look for points with easy access to deep water. Fish the tip as well as the corners for the best results.

TIP 28
Creek, Stream, or River Mouths

Most creek, stream, or river mouths that empty into or exit lakes or ponds are excellent areas to try for a variety of fish species.

Fish are often found in holes and drop-offs at the mouths, waiting for food coming into or out of the lake or pond.

TIP 29

Drop-Offs

Drop-offs are areas where the contour of the bottom rapidly drops to deeper water such as a hole or channel. Fish use these areas as migratory routes.

31

—————— TIP 30 ——————

Weed Cover

Weeds make prime cover for most species of fish, from small baitfish to large predators. Fish can be found in either deep-water submerged weed beds or shallow-water weed beds near the shore.

Many anglers mistakenly believe that during the hot summer months game fish can be found in the weeds because the water is cooler and the weeds provide shade. In actuality, the dense weed beds provide cover for game fish as they look for food. The water is actually warmer in densely weeded areas because the dark weeds absorb and radiate heat. Fish irregular weedline edges, open pockets, and the water above submerged weeds.

—————— TIP 31 ——————

Lily Pads

Don't overlook areas with lily pads. Even though they are difficult to fish, lily pads provide cover for all types of game fish.

Use a casting outfit and weedless lures when fishing pads, and work the edges and the pockets for the best results.

TIP 32

Weeds

Many game fish prefer specific types of weeds that they use for cover while searching for their next meal.

One of these weeds is cabbage, which is a favorite of the largemouth bass.

Cabbage

TIP 33

Reeds

Reeds are excellent areas to fish for bass or pike in early spring. Reeds that connect to marshy areas or are located at the mouth of a feeder creek provide excellent structure for fish.

Reeds

TIP 34

Weed Beds

Weeds are the most commonly found forms of structure in ponds, lakes, rivers, and streams. Some grow in the shallows, while other types grow in deep water. Knowing what type of weeds you're fishing in or around can be helpful when selecting the proper lure or bait.

Elodea   Milfoil   Cabomba

Coontail   Eel grass   Sand grass

TIP 35

Submerged Stumps

Submerged stumps make excellent areas to fish, depending on the amount of shade provided and access to deeper water or a breakline.

TIP 36

Submerged Brushpiles

Brushpiles are excellent areas to fish as both bass and crappies seek this type of cover. Work the cover from different angles.

If in deep water, try using jigs and live bait.

Brushpile

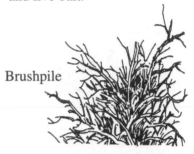

TIP 37

Submerged Trees

Sunken trees, stumps, and logs are excellent areas to look for crappies.

Try doing some jig fishing close in to the cover, using minnows or other live bait.

TIP 38

Bridges

Bridge supports are excellent fish-holding areas. The supports in rivers or streams create a natural holding area for fish as the current moves water and food past the supports.

Bridges also provide shade as cover for fish during the summer months.

TIP 39

Overhanging Trees

Overhanging trees provide shade that many game fish use as cover from the hot summer sun. Don't pass up trying these areas. Cast your offering along the edge of the shade at various angles.

TIP 40

Piers and Docks

Piers and docks are man-made structures that provide many species with cover from the sun. Lunker-size bass and pike are often found hanging around the posts or pilings in search of their next meal.

Cast as close as possible to piers and docks, trying different angles and lures. Also try a variety of live bait.

TIP 41

Riprap

Many man-made ponds, lakes, and reservoirs have shorelines covered with riprap, which is crushed rocks used to prevent shoreline erosion.

Try fishing areas where the riprap drops off into deep water. Many types of panfish and smallmouth bass prefer this type of structure.

TIP 42

Submerged Rockpiles and Boulders

In shallow water, rockpiles and boulders attract spawning fish. In deep water, they provide cover and are excellent areas to try for perch, saugers, or walleyes. Use a jig with live bait for the best results. Smallmouth bass, pike, and musky also like this structure.

TIP 43

Rocky Shorelines

Rocky shorelines, especially if they drop off to deep water, are ideal locations to find fish. Beneath the surface, rocky shorelines are broken and irregular, providing cover for baitfish as well as predators.

Fish as close as possible to the gaps among the submerged rocks, and you may hook a lunker hiding there.

TIP 44

Drains

Many communities have storm drains that either enter or exit nearby lakes, ponds, and lagoons. Along with stormwater runoff, all sorts of things, including food, enter or leave through the drains, attracting all sorts of fish.

Try fishing the edges of the discolored water for the best results.

TIP 45

Islands

Many lakes, ponds, rivers, and streams have islands that can be reached by boat or bridge. Fish islands the same way as any other shoreline, concentrating on the various forms of structure available.

TIP 46

Beaches

Many lakes with public beaches have sandy bottoms that provide excellent spawning areas during the spring.

Fish them in the early morning or late evening once the lakes have opened to the public. The beach areas contain vegetation that provides cover for predators in search for food. Try fishing the rafts and all sides of the weed edges using various lures or bait.

TIP 47

Fish as close as possible to the retaining wall since most fish will be holding tight against the wall.

Retaining Walls

Many homes on the water have retaining walls along the shore to prevent erosion caused by wind and water.

TIP 48
Old Roadbeds

Old roadbeds found in reservoirs or impoundments that were created when an area was dammed and flooded are excellent forms of structure used by various fish species as migratory routes.

To locate the old roads, try finding some old maps of the area prior to the flooding.

TIP 49
Steep Shorelines

Cliff-like shorelines, such as those found in strip mines or along some northern lakes and rivers, can be excellent productive locations for fishing.

In the strip mines, bass and walleyes can be found holding on ledges along the wall. When fishing this type of location, cast to the wall and allow your presentation to sink along the face before starting your retrieve.

TIP 50

Spillways and Dams

Spillways and dams can be found on rivers, streams, lakes, and ponds. Try fishing the area both above and below a spillway or dam.

Pools

Pools—areas formed at the base of a dam or spillway—often hold a lot of fish waiting for food to wash down from over the dam or spillway.

TIP 51

Eddies and Riffles

Eddies or riffles are formed when the current of a river or stream encounters some form of obstruction, causing the water to swirl around it.

Try fishing close to the object causing the eddy or riffle, as many fish lie in wait for their food there.

TIP 52

River or Streambeds

Reservoirs or impoundments are created when a river or stream is dammed up. Once the lake is formed, the old river or streambeds become the deepest waters in the lake, holding a large number of species of fish. To locate the beds or channels, try finding some old maps of the area prior to the flooding.

TIP 53
Boat Ramps

Boat launch ramps make for productive fishing areas. Deep water is close by, and in most cases, they have a sand or gravel bottom.

Try fishing these areas for panfish during the spring spawning season.

TIP 54
Deep Holes or Springs

Try fishing deep holes or springs where game fish may hold along the edges of the breakline or some species may suspend at middepth over the hole.

TIP 55
Undercuts

Undercuts, found along the banks of rivers and streams, are areas along the shore that have been washed away by the current, leaving an indentation under the bank.

Many types of fish hold in the undercuts waiting for the current to bring them their next meal. Fish the undercuts by allowing your presentation to drift downstream with the current as close to the shore as possible.

TIP 56

Spawning Areas

Spawning areas can be found in shallow bays and coves and along shorelines with sandy or gravel bottoms that have submerged weeds and deep water nearby.

Look for plate-size depressions in the sand or gravel to locate the beds.

TIP 57
Spawning Time

Most panfish (bluegills and sunfish) spawn during the months of May through August and sometimes as late as mid-September.

For some unexplained reason, bluegills spawn most frequently around a full moon. Look for their beds within five days of a full moon.

TIP 58

Logjams

Logjams occur in rivers and streams when the current washes fallen trees and branches into large piles of debris.

The jams provide cover for predators waiting for food to be washed down with the current. Logjams are excellent areas to try fishing if you don't mind losing a few lures to snags.

TIP 59

Location Markers

When you're out fishing in a boat and you find a hot spot that you want to come back to, drop a buoy marker to mark the spot. The marker can be made from a piece of styrofoam with a sinker tied to it with a string or length of line.

TIP 60

Reading the Water

Regardless of where they fish or what species they're after, successful fishermen have a few things in common.

Good fisherman have an ability to recognize details about the water they plan to fish. They study the water carefully to determine the conditions.

They ask themselves if the water is high, low, or average; if it is clear or muddy; if any structure is nearby. They also determine the best place the fish may be and what lure or bait would be best to use under these conditions.

Good fishermen leave very little to chance; they use common sense and experience to be successful.

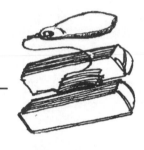

Chapter 3

Equipment Tips

The following pages contain tips on caring for basic equipment, knot tying, and miscellaneous information.

TIP 1

Cleaning Reels

Every fisherman should have the following tools when cleaning his or her fishing reels:

1. A small flat-blade jewelers' screwdriver for small screws.
2. A small Phillips screwdriver for Phillips-head screws.
3. A pair of long-nose pliers for removing and replacing tiny screws and parts.
4. A small flashlight or lamp to light up the inner workings of the reel.
5. A container to hold parts while cleaning or repairing.
6. A small kitchen strainer to hold parts as they are washed under hot water.

TIP 2

Polishing Reels

A tube of toothpaste and a little reel grease can be used as an abrasive compound to polish the inner parts of a reel, making it silky smooth, reducing backlashes and wear, and increasing distance casting.

Just dismantle the reel and pack in a 50/50 mixture of reel grease and paste in the gear area to be polished. Reassemble the reel, and manually wind the reel for about eight to twenty hours, periodically checking on the polishing compound. After the gears are polished, clean out the toothpaste with soap and water, and grease and oil all the parts.

TIP 3

Tackle Boxes

During the long winter months and prior to any fishing trip, check and clean your tackle box.

Take the time to dump everything from the box and clean it, using a mixture of water and baking soda. When dry, examine the items taken from the box for damage and repair, clean, or replace them, as necessary, before returning them to the tackle box.

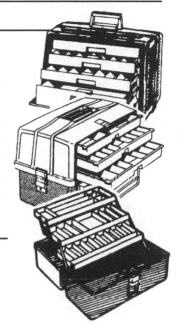

TIP 4

Line Snipper

A handy item to carry in your tackle box or to attach to your vest is a fingernail clipper. You can use it to clip off excess material when tying on hooks, snaps, swivels, lures, or flies.

TIP 5

Marking Pens

Permanent markers

Carry a set of permanent marking pens in your tackle box. You can use them to put streaks on spoons and plugs, cover jig heads so that they won't gleam in the sun, or mark a line when ice fishing without a bobber so that you can return to the same depth after you catch a fish.

TIP 7

Discarding Old Line

At one time or another, most fishermen must remove and discard a backlash or a bird's nest they get on the line on their reel.

Discarded nylon or monfilament lines degrade slowly and can be a danger to birds and other wildlife. A true sportsman will not leave this discarded line along the stream bank or lake shore or in the water. Put it in your pocket or vest until you can dispose of it in a garbage can.

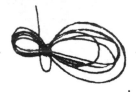

TIP 6

Purchasing Line

When purchasing fishing line, consider the following:
• The type of conditions you will be facing.
• The type of fish you are after.
• The type of equipment you will be using.

Then determine which of the following properties apply to your fishing needs: break strength, stretch, line uniformity, stiffness, abrasion resistance, and color.

Most line manufacturers list the above characteristics on their packaging. Read the information on the package to determine if the line meets your requirements.

TIP 8

Line Twist

To prevent line twist, use a good quality swivel. However, if your line does get twisted, try to untwist it with the following suggestions:
• First, remove anything at the end of the line (lures, swivels, and so forth).
• If boat fishing, let out all the line and troll it behind the boat.
• If stream or river fishing, let out all the line and let it drift downstream in the fast current.

TIP 9

Lure Cleaning

To give your chrome-plated spoons, spinner blades, and lures a new shine, use a mixture of vinegar and baking soda to rub out the tarnished, stained, dull look after a season of fishing.

TIP 10

Polishing Spoons

Restore the luster or shine to a dull spoon with a little elbow grease, a steel-wool pad, and some toothpaste.

Remove the grime with the steel wool, and use the toothpaste to polish the surface.

TIP 11

Modified Spoons and Spinners

Drilled holes

Drill a few holes in the rear section of a spoon or spinner blade to create a bubbling and low-hum effect that attracts fish. Drill $1/8$-inch holes in small spoons or blades and $1/4$-inch holes in the larger ones. The holes also allow the spinner blade to turn faster at a slower speed.

TIP 12

Adding Legs

If you fish with soft plastic body lures, here's a way to make them more effective.

Buy some living rubber from your local fly-fishing shop or sporting goods store, or use thin rubber bands.

Thread the rubber through the eye of a large sewing needle, and push the needle through the lure body to form a pair of legs.

If you want more legs, repeat the process with another piece of rubber.

TIP 13

Lure Tip

If the fish aren't biting at your favorite spinners, lures, or jigs, try adding a night crawler or a piece of pork rind to the hook.

Just make sure that it doesn't affect the action of the lure or spinners.

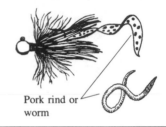

Pork rind or worm

TIP 14

Polka-Dot Lure

Try this trick if your spoons or spinners aren't producing. Buy a few small bottles of various colored lacquer paints from your local hobby shop. Then using the head of a flat-headed nail, add a bunch of different colored polka dots to the spoons and spinner blades.

TIP 15

Snagless Sinker

Make a snagless sinker with a piece of nylon cord, some bird shot or split shot, a candle or lighter, and a pair of pliers.

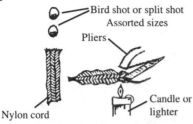

Bird shot or split shot Assorted sizes

Pliers

Candle or lighter

Nylon cord

First, take a short piece of the nylon cord, remove the inner threads, and grasp one end with the pliers. Using a candle or flame from a lighter, melt the nylon at the pliers to seal off the end.

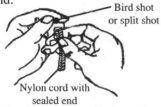

Bird shot or split shot

Nylon cord with sealed end

After the end cools, fill the nylon cord with enough bird shot or split shot to meet the desired weight you want and seal the open end with the candle or lighter. To finish the snagless sinker, make a hole at one of the sealed ends and attach a snap swivel.

Typical Snagless Rig

Swivel

Snelled hook

Snap swivel

Snagless sinker

TIP 16

Homemade Pencil Sinker

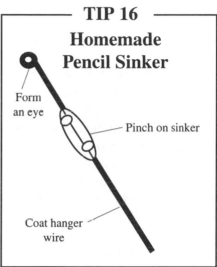

Form an eye

Pinch on sinker

Coat hanger wire

TIP 17

Sinker/Float Sizes

Rule of thumb
for which size to use

Float Size (Diameter in inches)	Sinker Size (Ounces)
1	$1/8$
$1\,1/4$	$1/4$
$1\,1/2$	$1/2$
$1\,3/4$	1
2	$1\,3/4$

TIP 18

Netting Fish

Before you reel the fish near to the boat or shore, get the net into the water. Hold the net at a 45-degree angle, and then lead the fish into it. As the fish enters the net, lift up and out of the water.

Never try to net the fish from the tail end or scoop it into the net. Take your time, and lead it headfirst into the net.

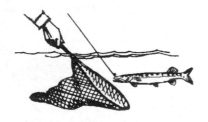

TIP 19

No-Sink Net

Try this tip to make sure your net will float if it ever falls or is knocked into the water while trolling. Purchase an aerosol can of styrofoam insulation from your local hardware or home improvement store. Remove the end cap on the net, and spray the foam into the hollow handle.

Be sure to fill it with enough foam so that the net will float.

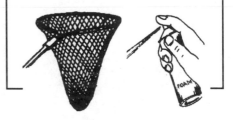

TIP 20

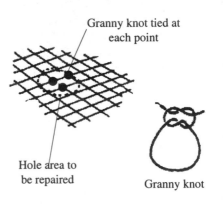

Granny knot tied at each point

Hole area to be repaired

Granny knot

Net Repairs

If you rip a hole in your net, try making a simple repair by "granny knotting" the hole or snag.

Use a six-pound mono line to tie a granny knot at each point of the tear or snag.

— TIP 21 —

Catch-and-Release Fishing Hooks

Catch-and-release is a popular practice on many lakes and streams throughout the country. While many catch-and-release anglers use barbless hooks, you can also use a regular hook if you file or mash the barb down with a pair of pliers.

A filed-down hook requires a tight line to land your catch, but it also means less injury to the fish when you release it.

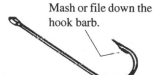

Mash or file down the hook barb.

TIP 22

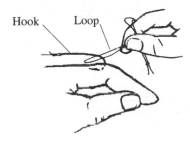

Hook   Loop

Removing a Hook

To remove a hook from your hand, form a 10-inch loop with a piece of line, and tie the ends together. Slip your free hand up to the wrist into the loop and grasp the looped line between your thumb and forefinger.

Place the loop over the embedded hook eye and center it in the middle of the hook bend. Hold the hooked hand still, and with the loop hand, apply pressure down and back with a sharp jerk of the loop. The hook will pop out the same hole it entered.

— TIP 23 —

Dull Hooks

While dull hooks often cause you to lose fish, few anglers take the time to inspect and sharpen their hooks.

All types of hones and sharpening devices are available at many sporting goods stores at a reasonable price.

It's a good practice to carry a hook-sharpening device in your tackle book to keep your hooks sharp while fishing.

TIP 24

Rod Guide Repairs

If the tip or guides on your rod become grooved, try this before you go out and buy new replacements.

All you'll need is a variable drill, a few cotter pins ($^3/_{32}$ to 2 inch) and some emory cloth. Cut a $^1/_2$-inch to 1-inch piece of emory cloth, and cover and slide it into the center of the cotter pin. Insert the pin into the drill chuck and then into the guide, and slowly grind down the groove.

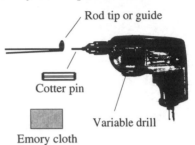

Rod tip or guide

Cotter pin

Variable drill

Emory cloth

TIP 25

Loose-Fitting Ferrules

If you have a rod with a loose-fitting ferrule, you can fix it by applying some beeswax or wax from an ordinary household candle to the male end of the ferrule.

If you don't have any wax, place a few hairs from your head upright in the female ferrule before inserting the male ferrule.

These are only temporary solutions, and you should replace the ferrules with new ones.

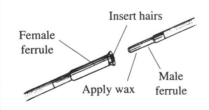

Insert hairs

Female ferrule

Apply wax

Male ferrule

TIP 26

Repairing Cork Rod Grips

If your favorite cork rod grip has a few chunks torn out or missing, try this.

Take a cork from a wine bottle, and cut a piece large enough to fit in the missing area. Use sandpaper or a file to make some cork sawdust with the remaining part of the cork, and mix it into some wood glue. Fill the hole with the mixture, insert the cork piece, and allow it to dry. After it dries, sand it down to a smooth finish.

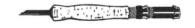

Every fisherman has an assortment of snaps and swivels, which at times end up loose in the lure compartments or the bottom of the tackle box.

The following are a few tips on snap and swivel use, and how to store them conveniently so that you can find them the next time you need them.

TIP 28

Storage Container

Empty 35-mm film containers can be used to hold snaps and swivels.

Label the containers with a piece of tape and a marking pen and either store in your tackle box or carry them in your pocket while fishing.

TIP 27

Storing Snaps and Swivels

Here's a simple tip to keep your snaps and swivels in one place. Put them on a paper clip or on a safety pin.

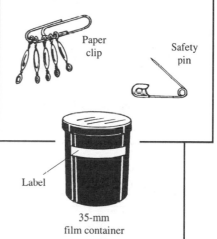

Paper clip

Safety pin

Label

35-mm film container

TIP 29

Snaps

If you want a quick, easy way to change hooks or lures, use a snap at the end of your line.

Assorted snaps

TIP 30

Swivels

When casting lures or fishing in a current, use a swivel at the end of your line to prevent your lure or bait from twisting. Keep an assortment of different sizes and types in your tackle box.

Assorted swivels

TIP 31
Bobber Selection

Bobbers or floats serve two purposes: They are made to keep the bait off the bottom, and they are used to indicate when a fish is biting. Select bobber type and size to match the type of fish you're after and the equipment and bait you're using.

TIP 32
Bobber Stop Knot

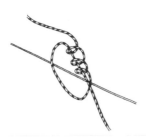

Using Dacron line, tie a loose square knot around your mono line. Take one end of the Dacron line and run it in and out of the loop several times and then pull both ends tight. Snip off any excess Dacron.

TIP 33
Bobber Stop-Line/Thread Knot

Here's a simple way to make a bobber stop with a piece of line or thread. Take an 18-inch piece of line or thread, and lay it alongside your fishing line. Wrap the second end back over the fishing line (forming a loop) to where you started. Wrap over all three strands about four or five turns going back toward the loop.

At the last turn, pass the second end through the loop and pull both ends of the line or thread tight. Clip off the remaining ends, and slide the line to the desired spot on the fishing line.

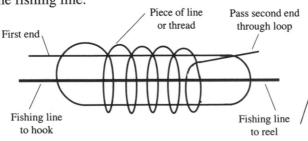

First end — Piece of line or thread — Pass second end through loop — Fishing line to hook — Fishing line to reel

TIP 34

Hook Remover

To make a simple hook remover, take a 6-inch-long piece of aluminum tubing, which you can buy in a hobby shop or hardware store, and cut a slit along the side with a hacksaw.

When using it, slip your line into the slit and slide the tube down to the hook. Keep the line tight, and with a little push, you can disengage the hook.

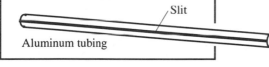
Slit

Aluminum tubing

TIP 35

Carryall

Old golf bags make great carryalls if you're a bank or shore fisherman.

You can put your rods or poles where the golf clubs went and your other equipment in the ball compartments.

You can also go first class if you use a pull cart for the bag.

TIP 36

Safety Pin Applications

Safety pins can be a handy item to have in your tackle box. They can be used to store hooks and swivels or as an emergency rod guide or rod tip.

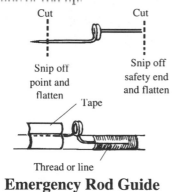

Cut   Cut

Snip off
point and
flatten

Snip off
safety end
and flatten

Tape

Thread or line

Emergency Rod Guide

Storage

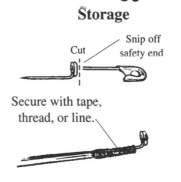

Cut

Snip off
safety end

Secure with tape,
thread, or line.

Emergency Rod Tip

TIP 37

Bank-Fishing Rod Holder

If you do a lot of bank fishing and you use more than one pole, make yourself a few of the following rod holders.

Buy a length of PVC plastic pipe from your home improvement or hardware store, and cut it into 16-inch pieces with one end cut at a 60-degree angle.

When fishing, drive the angled end into the bank at a 45-degree angle, cast out your line, and insert the rod handle into the holder.

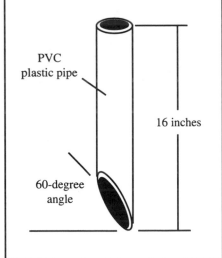

PVC plastic pipe

16 inches

60-degree angle

TIP 38

Polarized Sunglasses

If you use sunglasses while fishing, buy a pair with polarizing lenses. They improve your underwater vision, allowing you to spot fish and observe bottom conditions.

TIP 39

Casting Bubble

If you want to cast flies using your spinning outfit rather than a fly rod, get a few casting bubbles. They can be filled with water to control distance and depth and are simple to attach to your line.

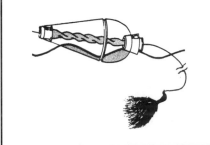

Braid Knot

This knot is used to connect hooks, swivels, lures, etc.

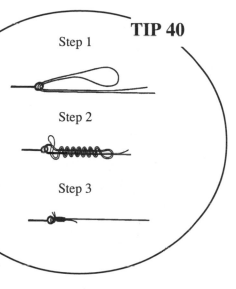

TIP 40

Step 1

STEP 1. Run a loop through the eye of a hook, swivel, lure, etc.

Step 2

STEP 2. Run the loop around the line eight times, bringing the loop back and threading it between the eye and the coils.

Step 3

STEP 3. Tighten the knot with a steady, even pull, and trim the loop, leaving about $1/4$ inch.

TIP 41

Jam Knot

This knot is used to connect swivels, hooks, and snaps to the end of a line.

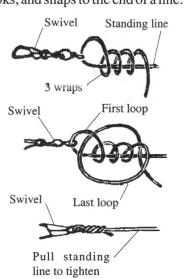

STEP 1. Pass the line through the eye of the swivel and make three wraps over the standing line.

Swivel   Standing line

3 wraps

STEP 2. Bring the working end around through the first loop and then thru the last loop.

Swivel   First loop

STEP 3. Holding the loops with the fingers of one hand, pull slowly on the standing line with the other hand to tighten the knot.

Swivel   Last loop

Pull standing line to tighten

Joining Lines

If you can tie a shoelace, you can tie this no-slip knot to join two lengths of fishing lines.

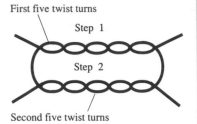

First five twist turns

Step 1

Step 2

Second five twist turns

STEP 1. Make five twist turns with the two pieces of line as shown.

STEP 2. With the loose ends, make the second five twist turns as shown.

STEP 3. Pull up the ends of each line, drawing them tight as shown.

Step 3

STEP 4. After the knot's tight, clip off the remaining loose ends.

Step 4

TIP 43

Double through the Eye Clinch Knot

STEP 1. Pass the line through the hook or lure eye, and double back through the eye a second time.

STEP 2. Make six wraps around the standing line.

STEP 3. Bring the end of the line back to the eye, and pass it between the eye and the first wrap.

STEP 4. Tighten with a steady pull and trim the ends.

TIP 44

Yarn Tie

Use this tie to hold a piece of yarn on the hook when steelhead or salmon fishing.

STEP 1. Slip the line through the hook eye along the hook shank.

STEP 2. Holding the line along the shank, make about four loose wraps up the shank toward the hook eye.

STEP 3. Bring the tag end through the four loose wraps and slowly tighten the line with an even, steady pull.

TIP 45

Eye Knot

Pass the line twice through the eye, forming two loops, and then pass the end through both loops and tighten.

TIP 46

Rolling Splice

Make about six loose wraps of the lighter line around the heavier line, pass the end through half the loose wraps, and tighten.

TIP 47

Double Turle Knot

Pass the line through the eye of a hook, snap, swivel, lure, or fly and make a loop with the line. Bring the end around and through the loop, and again pass the end twice more through the loop as shown.

Pass the loop over the hook, snap, swivel, lure, or fly, and draw the line tight so that it closes snug at the eye.

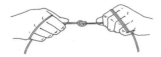

TIP 48

Trilene Knot

Use this knot to connect hooks, swivels, lures, etc.

Tag end

STEP 1. Run the line through the eye of a hook, swivel, lure, etc., and double back through the eye a second time.

5 to 6 loops

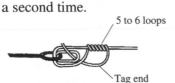

Tag end

STEP 2. Make five to six loops with the tag end of the line around the standing line, and then bring it back and thread it between the eye and the coils.

Tag end

STEP 3. Tighten the knot with a steady, even pull, and trim the tag end leaving about $1/4$ inch.

TIP 49

Simplified Snell Knot

Here's an easy way to make your own snelled hooks.

Tag end

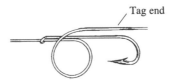

STEP 1. Run about 6 inches of the tag end of the line through the eye of the hook, holding the line against the hook shank, and form a circle or a loop.

Tag end

STEP 2. Make as many turns through the circle or loop and around the line and shank as you need. Close the turns by pulling on the tag end of the line.

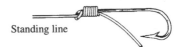

Standing line

STEP 3. Finish the knot by pulling the standing line in one direction and the hook in the opposite direction.

TIP 50

Overhand Knot

Use this simple knot to join two lines together or to form a loop. Simply take the lines and form a loop, passing one end through the loop and pulling both ends tight.

Chapter 4

Bait Tips

This chapter contains tips on using live bait when freshwater fishing. The tips cover all types of live bait and how to purchase, catch, care for, and use them.

TIP 2

Aeration

When you purchase your minnows, also buy oxygen tablets to add to your bait bucket.

The tablets will keep your bait alive until you reach your destination and put them into the lake or stream.

── TIP 1 ──
How Much to Buy

Never overcrowd a bait bucket without proper aeration. The following is the maximum number of various baitfish to buy when the water you plan to fish has a temperature of 50 degrees or less.

Shiners	2 dozen
3-inch fatheads	3 dozen
3-inch dace	3 dozen
3 inches + dace	1 dozen
Creek chubs	1 dozen
Suckers	1 dozen

When the water temperature is 55 degrees or more, cut the number in half.

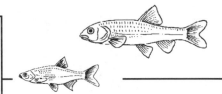

── TIP 3 ──

Minnow Fishing

When minnow fishing, use a small, light hook made of fine wire, and run the hook through the lips of the minnow.

── TIP 4 ──
Discarding Bait

When you're done fishing and you have some bait left, don't dump it into the lake or stream. If you have a live well at home, take them with you when you leave. If you don't want them, toss them into the trash can or on the ground.

TIP 5
What to Buy

The following is a basic guideline for what type of fishing baitfish to use and the bait size to use for them.

Type of Baitfish		Used for	Size (in inches)
Alewife		Trolling/casting: salmon, trout	3–6
Golden Shiner		Still/trolling: bass, perch, pickerel, northerns, muskie, walleye, trout	3–7
Fathead Minnow		Still/trolling/casting: all species	2–3
Bluntnose Minnow		Still/casting: all species	2–3$\frac{1}{2}$
Creek Chub		Still/casting: bass, northerns, muskie, walleye	3–8
Gizzard Shad		Still/trolling/casting: bass, catfish	4–12
Sucker		Still/trolling/casting: bass, northerns, trout, walleye	6–12
Dace		Still/trolling/casting: bass, northerns, muskie, walleye	3–4
Mud Minnow		Still/casting: all species	2–4
Madtom		Still/casting: northerns, walleye, catfish, bass	2–4

TIP 6
Shiners

1$\frac{1}{2}$-inch to 2-inch shiners are the number one bait for crappies and perch.

TIP 7
Purchasing Minnows

When purchasing minnows, make sure they are swimming together and near the bottom or corner of the tank.

63

TIP 8

Selecting Worms

The following is a basic guide-line for selecting what type of worm to use when fishing.

Night crawler (7 to 10" long)
Easy to find; great for bass, catfish; sold in most bait shops.

Garden worm (3 to 4" long)
Excellent panfish bait; common in flower beds.

Leaf worm (3 to 4" long)
Great for most species; found in compost piles or decaying leafs.

Manure worm (3 to 4" long)
Excellent bait for crappie, bluegills, trout; found on farms or local stables.

Wiggler (2" long)
Best panfish bait; sold in most bait shops or found on farms or stables.

TIP 9
Worm Care

If you use your own supply of worms, keep them lively and frisky by feeding them coffee grounds or scraps of lettuce, and give them a 1-inch cube of mar-garine.

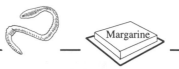

TIP 10
Worm Container

Make a worm container from any can with a plastic lid (like a coffee can). Collect a couple of the same type of cans, save the lids, and remove the bottom from one of the empty containers. (You will need both lids but only one container.)

Place the lids on both the top and bottom of the can, and put your worms into the container. This way, while fishing you will be able to easily retrieve your worms from either end of the container.

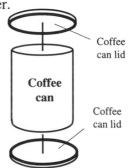

Coffee
can lid

**Coffee
can**

Coffee
can lid

TIP 11

Coffee Can Container

Fill a 1-pound coffee can with a snap-on plastic lid three-fourths full with shredded newspaper. Place about thirty worms on top of the shredded paper, and snap on the lid. The can with the worms can go to a cool place or a refrigerator, where they will stay nice and fresh for a couple of weeks or longer.

TIP 12

Rainstorm Collecting

When you anticipate a thunderstorm or heavy rain, place some flat pieces of styrofoam or board on the ground, weighing them down with a rock so that they don't blow away.

After the rain ends, lift up the boards or styrofoam and pick up the worms under them.

TIP 13

Walnut Magic

If you buy walnuts in the hull, save the hulls and use them to collect worms.

Fill a 5-gallon bucket one-third full with walnut hulls and the rest with water. Let it stand for a few days, stirring it once a day.

When the grass is wet after a shower and the worms are near the surface, pour the solution into a sprinkling can and spread it over an area where you want to collect worms. The caustic solution will force the worms to the surface, where you can pick them up.

TIP 14

Fishing with
Grasshoppers and Crickets

Grasshoppers and crickets serve as good bait for many species of fish. The best place to hook a hopper or cricket is just behind the head.

If you have any left after a day of fishing, try freezing them. Any small container that takes up little room in the freezer, such as a butter tub or a plastic baggie, can be used to hold them. You will appreciate the frozen hoppers or crickets later in the year when live ones become scarce.

TIP 15
Crickets

Crickets are raised commercially in many areas as bait. If you can't buy live crickets at your local bait shop, try the local pet shop. Pet shops carry live crickets as food for pet turtles and lizards.

You can also catch your own by turning over logs, stones, or boards in the field or by using traps baited with bread, bread crumbs, and sugar. Crickets can be kept in a vented container (with air holes) with grass clippings for several weeks.

TIP 16

Grasshoppers

Grasshoppers are an excellent bait for panfish but are often overlooked as a bait because they aren't sold in most bait shops. Next time you plan to go fishing in the summer, take a walk to an empty weedy field and catch a few hoppers to take along. You'll be surprised by the results.

TIP 17

Fishing with Frogs and Tadpoles

Frogs and tadpoles, a popular bait for decades, are most often used to catch largemouth bass.

Both mature frogs and tadpoles are sold in bait shops, but they also can be caught in many lakes and ponds in the spring months.

TIP 18

Fishing with Toads

Toads can also be used as bait for a number of game fish species. However, toads are difficult to obtain and are rarely sold in bait shops.

If you live in an area where toads are common, try catching your own. Toads should be fished the same way as frogs or salamanders.

TIP 19

Fishing with Salamanders

Using salamanders as bait is becoming more popular in many parts of the country.

More than 100 species of salamanders live in water or on land in North America. Three types are most frequently used as bait: mole, giant, and lungless salamanders. The larvae of these salamanders are called "water dogs" and are often sold in bait shops. They make an excellent bait for a number of game fish species and are one of the easiest baits to keep alive.

TIP 20

Leech Identification

The illustrations to the right are examples of various types of leeches found in North America. Of the four leeches shown, the ribbon leech is most widely used as bait, followed by the tiger leech. The horse leech and the medicine leech are the least effective as a bait and should be avoided.

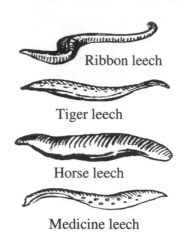

Ribbon leech

Tiger leech

Horse leech

Medicine leech

TIP 21

Purchasing or Catching Leeches

Leeches are mostly sold in bait shops throughout the northcentral states. They are one of the best baits for walleye and largemouth bass.

When buying leeches, look for firm, lively, and spunky ones. Leeches can also be caught in many ponds and lakes by using a coffee can or gunnysack baited with fish heads or beef kidneys.

TIP 22

Best Walleye Bait

Leeches are the most popular walleye bait used in the northcentral states. Because of their effectiveness, some resorts have tried to have them banned as a bait.

Leeches are seldom used in the southern part of the country, but it may be worth giving them a try if you live or visit the south.

When using leeches as bait, be sure to change them frequently.

TIP 23

Keeping Leeches

Start with about a pound of healthy leeches in a plastic, foam, or glass container approximately 12 inches square. (You should be able to obtain them from a bait shop or by catching your own.)

Keep them in clean, fresh, nonchlorinated water and store them in a refrigerator at 40 to 45 degrees.

Do not feed them, and clean the container every five days to control the mucus or slime they produce when they are disturbed. They will keep for months, giving you a good ready supply of bait.

12 inches square

TIP 24

Removing Leeches

To remove a leech from your body, use a little garlic or beer. Crushed garlic smeared on a leech will kill it, while a little beer (not surprisingly) will make the leech erratic and easy to remove.

TIP 25

Handling Leeches

If you don't like to handle leeches, put a rock in your bait bucket along with your leeches. They will attach themselves to the rock, making them easier to hook.

Simply lift the rock out of the bucket and hook the leech while it's attached to the rock. Remember to hook the fat part of the leech, just behind the sucker.

TIP 26

Acorn Grubs

Acorn grubs, the larvae of the nut weevil, are an excellent panfish bait. They can be found under oak trees in the acorns lying on the ground.

The telltale sign of the acorn holding a grub is the small hole made in the side of the nut. The grubs are cream colored and are about $^1/_4$ inch long. They are also an excellent bait for ice fishing.

TIP 27

Wood Borers

Wood borers, the larvae of the june bug, can be found by digging in the black soil under rotting logs.

They are white with black heads, crescent shaped, and grow to about 1 inch in length. They are an excellent bait for panfish all year long.

TIP 28

Paper Wasp Larvae

Wasp larvae are off-white colored and grow up to 1 inch in length. An excellent ice fishing bait for panfish, they should be collected in the winter months when the adults are dormant.

A single hive can produce dozens of larvae. Be sure to open the hive outside in a cold area.

TIP 29

Wax Worms

Wax worms, the larvae of the wax bee moth, can be purchased in most bait shops. If you know any beekeepers, you may want to ask them for their old or unused hives, as wax worms are found in the hive cells or in the debris on the bottom.

The larvae are cream colored with a red head, are crescent shaped, and grow to about 1 inch in length. They are an excellent bait for panfish all year long.

TIP 30

Goldenrod Grubs

Goldenrod grubs, the larvae of the gall moth, can be found in goldenrod plants with a swelling in the stem.

The grubs are white with a black head, crescent shaped, and about the size of a popcorn kernel. They are an excellent bait for panfish all year long.

TIP 31

Meal Worms

Meal worms, the larvae of the darkling beetle, can be purchased at most pet shops. If you have a grain elevator near you, that's another good place to find them.

They are yellow/brown in color and about 1 inch in length. They are an excellent bait for panfish all year long.

TIP 32

Maggots

Maggots, the larvae of flies, are sold in many bait shops.

They are cream colored and grow to about $1/2$ inch in length. They are an excellent bait for panfish all year long.

TIP 33

Caterpillars

Many moths and butterfly larvae can be used for bait. The catalpa worm is one example commonly used in the south.

Other larvae that make good bait and are more easily found are tent caterpillars, webworms, corn earworms, and cutworms. All of those caterpillars make excellent bait for panfish and can be collected with little difficulty near one's home.

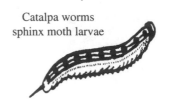

Catalpa worms
sphinx moth larvae

TIP 34

Aquatic Insects

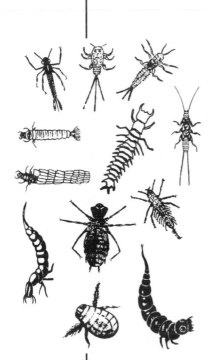

Most insects that make up a fish's diet are aquatic. Every stream, river, and lake contains some form of aquatic life that can be caught and used as bait.

To get a nice supply of bait, try turning over a few rocks in a stream, pulling out a handful of weeds, or scooping through the weeds or along the bottom with a net.

Insect larvae or nymphs from an alderfly, mayfly, stonefly, caddisfly, dobsonfly, damselfly, dragonfly, or water beetle can be found in most waters.

The next time you run low on bait while fishing, just look right in the water you're on. You'll be surprised at what you will find.

TIP 35

Crayfish

Found in most ponds, lakes, streams, and rivers, crayfish are a major part of the diet of both the largemouth and smallmouth bass. Crayfish can be purchased from most bait shops or caught with simple traps baited with liver or fish heads. They are an excellent bait for perch in smaller sizes as well as other panfish.

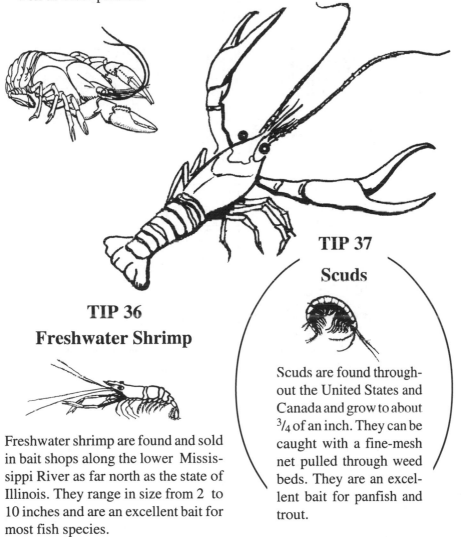

TIP 37

Scuds

Scuds are found throughout the United States and Canada and grow to about $3/4$ of an inch. They can be caught with a fine-mesh net pulled through weed beds. They are an excellent bait for panfish and trout.

TIP 36

Freshwater Shrimp

Freshwater shrimp are found and sold in bait shops along the lower Mississippi River as far north as the state of Illinois. They range in size from 2 to 10 inches and are an excellent bait for most fish species.

If you live near a creek, stream, river, or lake, you can catch your own bait by building and using a homemade bait trap. Diagrams on how to build your own are shown below. However, before you do it, check with your local authorities to see if it's legal to trap bait in your area.

TIP 38

Cylindrical Trap
⅛-Inch Wire Mesh

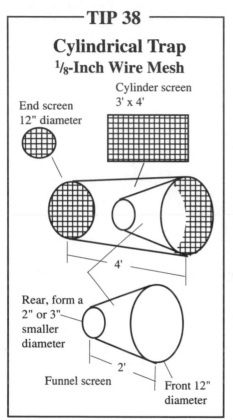

Cylinder screen
3' x 4'

End screen
12" diameter

4'

Rear, form a
2" or 3"
smaller
diameter

2'

Funnel screen

Front 12"
diameter

TIP 39

Box Trap
⅛-Inch Wire Mesh

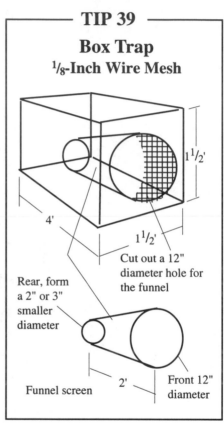

$1\frac{1}{2}$'

4'

$1\frac{1}{2}$'

Cut out a 12"
diameter hole for
the funnel

Rear, form
a 2" or 3"
smaller
diameter

2'

Funnel screen

Front 12"
diameter

TIP 40

Trap Baits

Baits to use depend on what baitfish you want to catch. For crayfish, use beef or pork liver. For minnows, use bread or dog biscuits. For leeches, use pieces of fish.

However, you never know what will turn up in your trap. You may catch all of the above.

Dog Biscuit

TIP 41

Catching Crayfish

Crayfish are often found in shallow water at night. To catch them, use a flashlight to spot them and a coffee can to trap them. Cut the top and bottom from a coffee can. When you see a crayfish, put the can over it to prevent the crayfish from escaping.

Remove top

Coffee

Remove bottom

TIP 42

Keeping Crayfish

Soft-shelled crayfish should be stored in a bait bucket filled halfway to the top with grass or aquatic weeds and a few ice cubes.

TIP 43

Crayfish Fishing

To fish for crayfish, you will need some raw liver, a piece of string, and an empty coffee can. Tie the liver to a 10-foot-long piece of string and toss it out into the water. Also submerge the coffee can in the water.

Wait a few minutes before pulling the string very slowly toward you. If you have a crayfish at the other end, you will feel it. Keep pulling the string slowly until you can see the crayfish, then grab the coffee can and work the crayfish in front of it. When the crayfish sees you, it will swim backwards into the can.

TIP 44

Scent Attraction

If you're a live-bait fisherman, here's a tip to try with artificial plastic or rubber worms, crayfish, and so on.

Store your artificial bait overnight with your live bait (night crawlers, wigglers, crayfish, and so forth). The artificials will pick up the natural scent of the live bait, making them more attractive to the fish.

TIP 45
More Scent Attraction

Add about ten to twenty drops of your favorite fish attractant in a resealable plastic bag with your plastic or soft-bodied baits.

Knead the baits in the bag to distribute the attractant to the plastic lures, which will absorb the attractant scent.

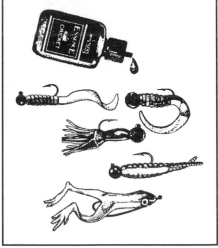

TIP 46

Livewell Bait Holder

If you own a boat with a livewell, here's a tip to keep your minnows or other live bait lively and easy to handle. Buy an inexpensive, rectangular-shaped, plastic, bathroom-size wastebasket, and drill several small holes in it. Keep it and the bait in your water-filled livewell.

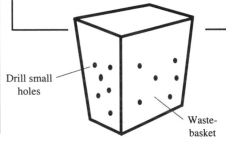

Drill small holes

Wastebasket

76

TIP 47

Throat Bait

The next time you clean a lot of fish, save the following as a jig dressing:

Cut out the throat tissue of the fish as shown below, and freeze it for later use.

When you use it, hook it at the front of the tissue.

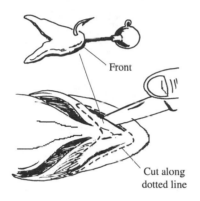

Front

Cut along
dotted line

TIP 48

Belly Bait

Another thing to do when cleaning fish is to cut a few strips $1/8$ inch wide and about $1/2$ inch long from the belly area.

Freeze them for later use, as they make an excellent bait for other game fish and panfish.

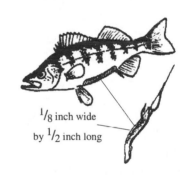

$1/8$ inch wide
by $1/2$ inch long

TIP 49

Dog Food Bait

Here's something new to try as a bait. Buy a box of Purina Chuck Wagon dog food, and separate the red nuggets from the yellow ones.

Give the yellow ones to your dog, and use the red nuggets on your next fishing trip. Wet the nuggets until soft, and then cut them with a knife in proportion to your hook size and quarry.

Fish the cut portions like a worm or catfish bait for the best results.

TIP 50

Tread Lightly

When looking for night crawlers, you'll get more faster if you wear sneakers and walk softly. Crawlers are very sensitive to vibrations, and the impact of stomping around while searching for them can drive them back into their holes.

TIP 51

Livelier Crawlers

Place your crawlers in a small container of soil that's been soaked overnight in red pickled beet juice. The crawlers will toughen up, be livelier, and have a red tint, making them more attractive to the fish.

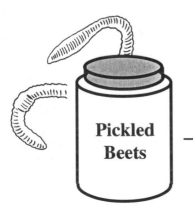

Pickled Beets

TIP 52

Catching Crawlers

When searching for crawlers at night after a soaking rain, place colored plastic wrap or a thin cloth over the lens of a flashlight, and secure it with a rubber band.

Too bright a light will send the crawlers swiftly into their holes.

TIP 53

Collecting Maggots

Liver — Wire

Coffee

Can

To collect maggots, place a piece of wire mesh with $1/4$ inch holes over a 3-pound coffee can with about an inch or two of cornmeal on the bottom.

Then put a piece of raw liver on the mesh and place the can outside in the sun. After a day or two, check the can for maggots that have fallen into the cornmeal.

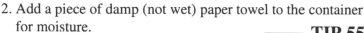

TIP 54

Keeping Maggots

After you purchase or raise your own maggots, do the following to keep them healthy and alive:

1. Use clean, dry sawdust as bedding.
2. Add a piece of damp (not wet) paper towel to the container for moisture.
3. Store them in the refrigerator.
4. Every week, take them out of the refrigerator and open the container and shake them for about 10 seconds.
5. Don't get them wet. Water will kill them.
6. Keep them out of the sun when fishing.

TIP 55

Bait Container

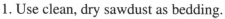

35-mm film cannisters make excellent containers for storing spikes, wax worms, grubs, or mealworms.

TIP 56

Freeze-Dried Baits

When fishing, it's a good idea to carry a few different types of freeze-dried bait as a backup.

Such bait as maggots, wax worms, grubs, and mealworms are currently available in most bait shops. They are easy to carry and work great if you run out of the live variety.

TIP 57

Single Worm

A single worm on a small hook works better than a big blob of worms on a large hook.

TIP 58

Covering the Hook

When you bait a hook, you don't have to cover up the point of the hook. Fish don't seem to mind if the point of the hook shows.

TIP 59

Hooking Baitfish

When using minnows or other types of baitfish, try hooking them ahead of the tail fin just below the backbone.

When fishing with them, lift them to the surface, making them splash on top, and then allow them to swim down. This will attract predators to the bait.

TIP 60

Early Morning Fishing

If you want an early start fishing and the bait shops will be closed when you get there, buy your bait the day before you go. You can keep minnows overnight if you store them in a cool place. Keep your worms or other bait in the refrigerator until morning.

Chapter 5

Presentation Tips

This chapter contains tips on presentation and covers a variety of methods for presenting your offerings and improving your chances of catching fish.

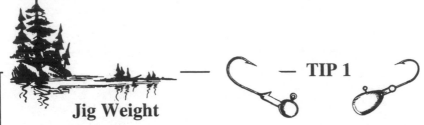

— **TIP 1**

Jig Weight

Jigs are designed to be fished on or near the bottom. Consider water depth, current, and wind when selecting the weight of the jig you intend to use. Use common sense when you make your selection. If you don't feel the bottom when fishing with a jig, try a heavier jig.

Line Test

TIP 2

The recommended line test for jig fishing follows:

Jig Weight	Line Test
$1/8$ oz. or lighter	4 lb.
$1/8$ to $1/4$ oz.	6 lb.
$1/4$ to $5/8$ oz.	8–10 lb.

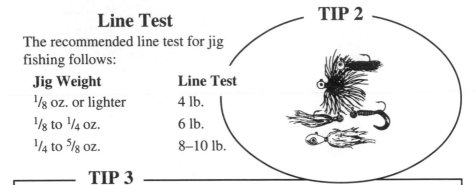

TIP 3

Jig Presentation

After you cast, let the jig fall to the bottom before starting your lift-and-drop rod action. Always try to keep contact with the bottom during the retrieve. Become a line watcher and be alert; any line movement can be a strike or a pickup. Many hits occur on the drop or fall of the jig, so be prepared to set the hook whether it's by feel or sight.

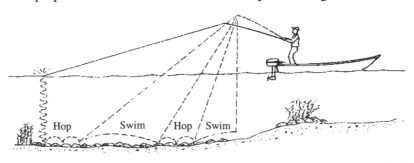

Hop Swim Hop Swim

TIP 4

Jig Presentation

Whether you use a jig baited with a minnow or another type of baitfish, your jig should imitate a nose-down feeding baitfish to be effective.

Predators are accustomed to seeing baitfish in a feeding position, and if your presentation is correct, it will fool them into striking your offering.

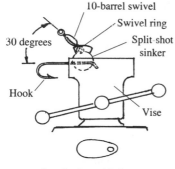

Materials

- 1 hook
- 5 or 7 "water gremlin" split shot
- 10-barrel swivel
- 0 or 1 spinner blade
- 1/0 split ring

10-barrel swivel
Swivel ring
30 degrees
Split-shot sinker
Hook
Vise

0 or 1 spinner blade

TIP 5

Roadrunner Jig

Here's a neat little jig you can make that works great for vertical jigging.

STEP 1. Using a pair of pliers, fasten a "water gremlin" split-shot sinker to the hook shank just behind the hook eye with the ears on the top of the hook shank.

STEP 2. Next, insert the hook and split-shot sinker into a vise with the ears of the sinker above the hook shank.

STEP 3. Insert the ring from one end of a barrel swivel between the "water gremlin" ears, and secure it to the split shot by using pliers to pinch it between the ears. **Note:** The barrel swivel should be at a 30-degree angle to the hook shank.

STEP 4. Attach a split ring to the opposite end of the barrel swivel ring, and a spinner blade to the split ring. Your roadrunner jig is ready to use.

TIP 6

Loose Loop System

Here's a way to get more action from a 7 surface "Rapala" lure when fishing for smallmouth bass.

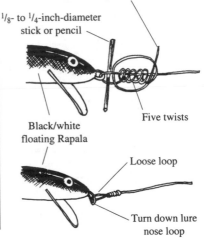

Slowly pull line up tight, and remove pencil or stick

$^1/_8$- to $^1/_4$-inch-diameter stick or pencil

Five twists

Black/white floating Rapala

Loose loop

Turn down lure nose loop

TIP 7

Spoon Tip

Try this when you're spoon fishing or trolling and the spoon action isn't right.

Remove the hook and swivel from the spoon, and reverse them. Attach the swivel at the wide end and the hook at the narrow end.

Doing this switch may or may not improve the action, depending on the type of spoon.

TIP 8

Modified Plastic Lures

To add more action to your soft-bodied plastic worms and tube lures, try the following: Take some dense-foam packing material, and cut it into small pieces. Stuff the pieces into the body cavity of the lure so that it floats upward when fished deep.

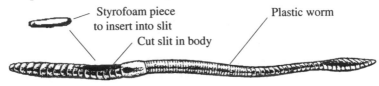

Styrofoam piece to insert into slit

Plastic worm

Cut slit in body

─── TIP 9 ───

Spinner Blades

Spinners with round Colorado-type blades work best when they are retrieved slowly while fishing in deep water.

Spinners with narrow willowleaf-type blades work best with a fast retrieve near the surface of shallow water.

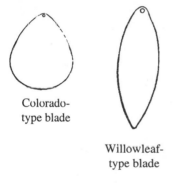

Colorado-type blade

Willowleaf-type blade

─── TIP 10 ───

Spinnerbaits

When fishing in clear water, use silver-bladed spinners with a white skirt. In stained waters, use gold-bladed spinners with a yellow or chartreuse skirt.

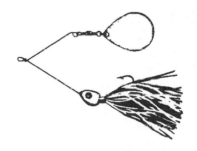

─── TIP 11 ───

Spinners

When a spinner isn't working, try adding a night crawler or a piece of pork rind to it. Just make sure your addition isn't too large that it affects the spinner's action.

TIP 12

Plastic Worm Colors

Of all the different colored plastic worms available today, the black and purple (grape) worms are the all-time favorites used by most worm fishermen. Other colors, such as translucent smoke or pale blue, work well in clear water, while darker colors, like motor oil or june bug, are best in muddy or murky water.

TIP 13

Added Action

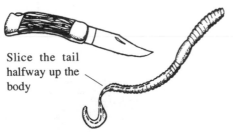

Slice the tail halfway up the body

To improve the action of your plastic worms, try the following: Using a razor blade or a sharp knife, slice halfway through the tail. This will give the worm more action when it sinks or when it's retrieved slowly with light jerks.

TIP 14

Plastic Worm Sizes

Selecting a plastic worm size depends on the type of fish you're seeking. Most fishermen prefer a 6-inch or longer worm when bass fishing and a 1- to 3-inch worm for panfish or small game fish.

Matching the worm with the proper hook is very important. For 4- to 6-inch worms, use a 1/0 or 2/0 hook. For 8-inch worms, use a 3/0 or 4/0 hook, and for 11-inch worms, use a 5/0 hook. For panfish or other game fish, use 1- or 3-inch worms and a 10, 8, or 6 hook.

TIP 15

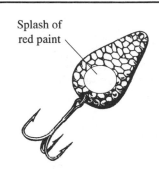

Splash of
red paint

Modified Lures

Add a splash of red paint to spoons or crankbaits or any lure with a rigid surface. The red color works as an attractor for hesitant fish when used in clear shallow water.

TIP 16

Modified Spinnerbait

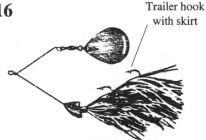

Trailer hook
with skirt

Add a second skirt to your spinnerbait by sliding a skirt over a trailer hook and adding it to the main hook by pushing it through the skirt's sleeve and the trailer's eye.

TIP 17

Modified Crankbait

Try this with a deep-running crankbait: Remove the rear hook from the crankbait, and add a split ring with a worm hook rigged with a plastic worm. You can also remove the forward hook if you're fishing weed beds. Removing the forward hook makes it almost weedless.

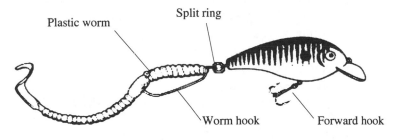

Plastic worm   Split ring

Worm hook   Forward hook

TIP 18

Jingle Bell

To add some sound to your worm rigs, place a small jingle bell between the nose of the plastic worm rigged on a worm hook and the bullet sinker. The bell can also be attached to other lures such as crankbaits, spoons, and spinnerbaits by using a split ring.

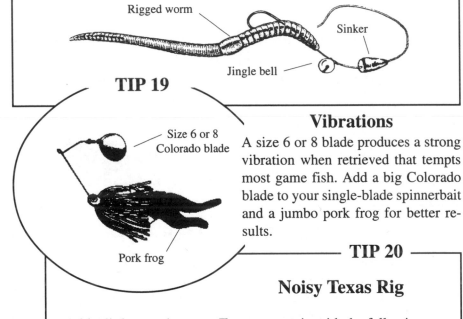

Rigged worm

Sinker

Jingle bell

TIP 19

Vibrations

Size 6 or 8
Colorado blade

A size 6 or 8 blade produces a strong vibration when retrieved that tempts most game fish. Add a big Colorado blade to your single-blade spinnerbait and a jumbo pork frog for better results.

Pork frog

TIP 20

Noisy Texas Rig

Add a little sound to your Texas worm rig with the following: Before the worm hook, slide a brass bullet-shaped weight on the line followed by a large glass bead. Rig your plastic worm on to the hook, and as you fish, twitch the rod rapidly, keeping the worm on the bottom. The action will make a clicking noise when the brass and glass come together.

Brass sinker

Glass bead

TIP 21

Pork Rind Fishing

Pork rind has been around for many years and can be purchased in assorted sizes and shapes. It can be used alone on a hook or as an enhancement to nearly any type of artifical bait. Next time you're out fishing, give it a try.

TIP 22

Pork Rind Storage

If you use pork rind as a trailer when you fish and the jar that holds the rind is too bulky for your vest or tackle box, try the following: Pack a few pieces along with a little of the brine in a small resealable plastic bag.

TIP 23

Pork Rind Presentation

Two things to remember when using pork rind:
First, pork rind should be used to enhance your lure, not overpower it. The amount you use is critical.
Second, pork rind can be cut and trimmed to match your lure size and to change the action.

TIP 24

Deep-Water Lure
Colors

When fishing deep water (over 20 feet), red-colored lures are less apt to attract fish. White and yellow lures are more effective because they appear larger and brighter in deep waters.

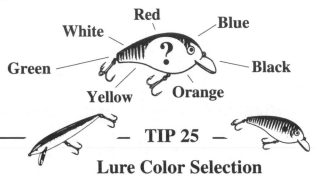

– TIP 25 –

Lure Color Selection

Many fishermen are unaware that the color of a lure may be completely different in the water than out of the water. While many colors will change according to the water depth, fluorescent colors show very little color change. When deciding on a lure color, consider the following information on what happens to colors underwater.

Lure Color

Water Surface	Black	White	Blue	Green	Yellow	Orange	Red
10' Deep	No Change	No Change	No Change	No Change	No Change	No Change	Rust
20' Deep	No Change	No Change	No Change	No Change	No Change	Rust	Brown
30' Deep	No Change	No Change	No Change	No Change	No Change	Rust	Brown
40' Deep	No Change	No Change	No Change	No Change	Pale Yellow	Dark Brown	Black
50' Deep	No Change	No Change	No Change	No Change	Pale Yellow	Dark Brown	Black
60' Deep	No Change	No Change	No Change	Pale Green	White	Black	Black

Chapter 6

Ice Fishing Tips

The following pages cover tips on ice fishing, ranging from safety on the ice to ways to improve your chances of catching fish.

TIP 1

First Ice

The first ice of the winter may be the most productive time to fish, but it can also be the most dangerous. Be extra careful with first ice. When you go out, take along a friend and wear a vest-type flotation device over your clothes. Also take along a 50-foot nylon rope in case you break through the ice and your friend has to pull you out.

TIP 2

Safety Tips

TIP 3

Vehicles on Ice

If you drive anything bigger or heavier than a snowmobile on to the ice, remember to move it to other locations from time to time.

Parking a vehicle such as a car or truck in one place tends to weaken the ice and increase the possibility of the ice breaking. It's safer to leave your vehicle on land and walk out to do your fishing.

When venturing out on the ice, remember these safety tips that could save your life:
1. Never go on to the ice if the ice is questionable.
2. Take along a partner.
3. Tell someone on shore where you plan to be.
4. Ice may be three feet thick in one place and only three inches thick a few feet away.
5. Clear new ice is stronger than clouded old ice with air bubbles in it.

TIP 4

Ice Fishing Checklist

Before you head out to do some ice fishing, make yourself a checklist so you don't forget anything. The following is an example of things you may want to put on the list:

☐ Insulated underwear
☐ Layered clothing
☐ Socks
☐ Insulated boots
☐ Hat
☐ Sunglasses
☐ Ice cleats
☐ Life vest
☐ Ice picks
☐ Five-gallon bucket
☐ Ice ladle
☐ Minnow bucket
☐ Bait
☐ Lures
☐ Auger or spud
☐ Depth finder
☐ Portable icehouse or tent
☐ Tip-ups
☐ Ice rods (jigging poles)
☐ Tell someone your location

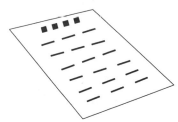

TIP 5

Where to Fish

There are no set rules for picking a location to make your holes for ice fishing. However, if you have a contour map of your favorite lake and you were successful at specific locations prior to it freezing, give them a try. If nothing happens in 30 minutes, move to another location.

TIP 6

Where to Start

Start on the breakline at 10 to 12 feet deep, setting tip-ups at 20, 25, and 30 feet deep. Rig your tip-ups with minnows or other types of bait, and keep the bait about 6 inches to 2 feet off the bottom.

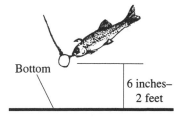

Bottom

6 inches–
2 feet

TIP 7

Best Bait

The best bait are the ones that catch fish; there are no set rules for selecting the best bait. However, the bait you choose will depend on the type of fish you're seeking and what it wants to eat.

Minnows, golden shiners, wax worms, and maggots or spikes are excellent as starters. Use maggots for panfish and minnows and shiners for larger game fish, such as walleyes and northerns.

When ice fishing, it's a good idea to have a variety of different bait and lures with you to try.

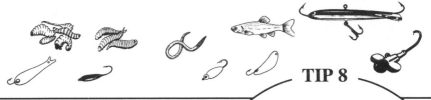

TIP 8

Finicky Panfish

For slow-biting finicky panfish, try a single grub or wax worm on a tiny hook rather than a gob of bait on a large flashy rig.

TIP 9

Panicky Bait

When fishing for northerns with a tip-up over a weed bed, make sure your bait can't hide in the weeds. Have only enough line out to keep your minnow or shiner 6 inches over the weeds.

6 inches

TIP 10
Fresh Grubs and Worms

To keep your worms and grubs warm and lively, place them in a small container inside your clothing.

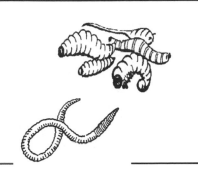

TIP 11

Fresh Minnows

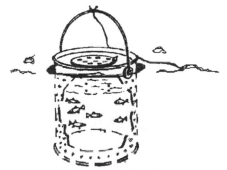

To keep your minnows fresh and to prevent them from freezing, make a separate hole in the ice that is big enough to hold your bait bucket.

The water under the ice is warmer than the surface air.

TIP 12

Fish Attractants

Try coating your bait with a fish attractant. Fish use their sense of smell to find food. Attractants disperse slowly in the cold water and entice finicky fish to take the bait.

TIP 13

Line Icing

Here are a few ways to reduce or eliminate icing on your fishing line. Run your line through a cloth saturated with mineral oil or through a folded piece of bacon fat. Not only does this slow down line icing, but it attracts fish to the bait.

TIP 14

Line Selection

For the best results while ice fishing, use a thin-diameter fishing line that will stay limp even in ice-cold water. Large-diameter line becomes stiff and unmanageable when cold.

The most commonly used line is 4- to 6-pound test, although 2-pound test works great for finicky panfish. Line color should be clear or green since those colors are the least visible.

TIP 15

Fine Line

At times, even 2-pound test line may be too heavy for finicky panfish.
On those days, attach a fly-fishing tippet material leader to your line.

Tippet material may be purchased at most tackle shops and comes in $1/2$-pound or $1/4$-pound test.

Also try reducing your hook and bait sizes, and you may just get those fussy panfish.

TIP 16

Cottage Cheese Attractor

I don't know if this works, but I read about it somewhere. Give it a try: Spread a few table-spoons of cottage cheese in the water, and wait a few minutes before you start fishing.

It's supposed to be a great attractor for pan-fish. I would think you would want the large curd.

Cottage Cheese

TIP 17

Button Attractor

Enlarge one of the holes on a small pearl button. When fishing deep dark water, hang the button on a hook or an ice fishing lure. Raise the hook or lure up and allow it to drop, causing the button to spin on the hook shank and attracting fish.

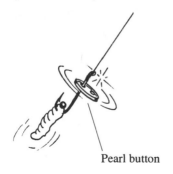

Pearl button

TIP 18

Bead Attractor

A few bright red beads strung on an 8 hook or an ice fishing lure work great for catching trout such as steelheads, browns, and lakers. The beads resemble spawn, fooling the trout into thinking they're get-ting a mouthful of salmon eggs.

Bright red beads

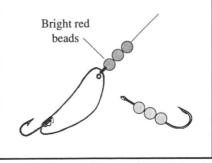

TIP 19

Cold Feet

To prevent cold or wet feet, try this trick: Slip a plastic bread bag over your stocking feet before putting on your shoes or boots.

Plastic bread bag

TIP 20

Take a Kid Ice Fishing

Ice fishing can be great fun for children who never tried it before. If you're involved with a scout group or some other community organization or if you want to teach your own kids how to ice fish, take them out on the ice.

Dress them warmly and comfortably, and go where you know you will probably catch fish. Most of all, try to make it a fun time.

TIP 21

Homemade Tip-Up
Materials

- Wood base
- Wood post, $2\frac{1}{2}$ to 3 feet long
- Nails
- Hanger wire
- Empty pop can
- Spool
- Bell sinker—must slide along wire

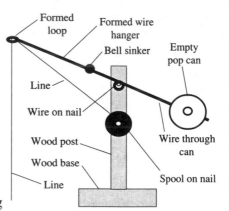

Formed loop

Formed wire hanger

Bell sinker

Empty pop can

Line

Wire on nail

Wood post

Wood base

Line

Wire through can

Spool on nail

TIP 22

Location

When fishing for panfish, remember that they seek warm water in the winter and cool water in the summer. Often, this will be the same place in the summer or winter.

If you know of a spot that worked in the summer, try it in the winter.

TIP 23
Catfish Bait

This bait only works in a lake or river with a good catfish population. Try this the night before you go out on the ice: Make little balls of bait about the size of your thumbnail from cat food. Let them dry out on a sheet of wax paper overnight, and then put them in a resealable plastic bag.

When on the ice, select a spot on the water that has little or no current to drill your holes. Drop a loose bait ball down each hole, and wait about ten minutes. After ten minutes or so, bait your rig with a grub or minnow, and drop it down to the bottom. You may catch other species, but if a catfish takes your bait, watch out. You'll be in for a surprise and some great action.

TIP 24

Shanty

An absolute must in spear fishing is a good dark shanty in which to sit.

TIP 25

Basic Spear Fishing

When spear fishing, anglers should wear dark clothes and gloves so that they are not visible to their underwater target. Holes for pike and muskie should be cut over water about 8 feet deep, and holes for sturgeon should be cut over water 10 to 20 feet deep.

Spears should be weighted for the type of fish that the angler is after. The spear should be attached to a line and lowered into the water before it is released. This eliminates any splash that may spook the fish.

Check your local fishing regulations for the spearing season.

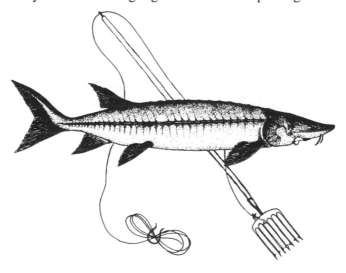

Chapter 7

Fly-Fishing Tips

The following tips on fly fishing cover safety as well as other information designed to improve your chances of catching fish.

TIP 1

No-Knot
Fly Attachment

If you have trouble tying knots when attaching your flies to a leader, check out a new gadget on the market called Fas-Snap. Manufactured by the Wilson Allen Corp., Fas-Snap makes attaching flies a snap. It is available in most sporting goods stores.

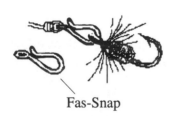

Fas-Snap

TIP 2

Line-to-Leader
Connection

If you are looking for an easy way to attach your leader to your fly line, try a Leader-Link made by Wright & McGill. They come in various sizes and make a strong, easy connection.

Leader-Link

TIP 3

No-Knot Eyelet

Another easy way to attach your leader to your fly line is to use a No-Knot Eyelet made by Nature Faker Inc. All you do is insert the eyelet into the hollow core of the fly line and tie your leader onto the eyelet.

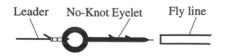

Leader   No-Knot Eyelet   Fly line

TIP 4

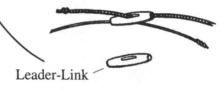

Recommended
Leader Sizes

Panfish	4X
Trout	4X or 5X
Bass	0X
Pike	0X
Salmon	0X

TIP 5
Stream Fishing

Start with a dry fly to see if the fish are feeding on the surface. If you don't get any rises after several casts, try a wet fly or go deep with a nymph pattern.

TIP 6

Fishing Small Streams

Never walk right up to a small stream. Keep a low profile, and wear drab clothing. Try making as little noise as possible to keep from spooking any fish in the area.

TIP 7
Fishing Big Streams

If you're fishing a big stream for the first time, cover a lot of water in search of deep pools. It will pay off.

TIP 8
Stream Fishing

Most fly fishermen wade into a stream without thinking. When approaching a stream, cover the close waters with a few casts before entering the water. Many fish often hold in water next to the bank or shoreline.

TIP 9
Insect Imitations

In addition to insects that lay their eggs in the water, fish also feed on land insects that find their way into the water by falling from overhanging trees or shoreline vegetation, or by being blown into the water by the wind.

These land insects are also a common part of a fish's diet and should be considered by the fisherman when preparing his or her arsenal of fishing lures.

It's a good idea to have a few ant, bee, grasshopper, or cricket imitations in your fly box the next time you're out on the water.

TIP 10
Matching the Hatch

To get a close look at the insects you capture in a stream, carry a small magnifying glass. Use it to look at your catch in detail, and then match your offering to the real thing.

TIP 11

Stream Insects

A good way to be successful when fishing a trout stream is to determine what life forms are floating or swimming downstream and match them with a fly.

To do this, hold a simple portable screen in the current for a few minutes to catch the critters in the water.

To make the screen, staple a 6-inch × 18-inch strip of nylon screen to 12-inch wooden handles.

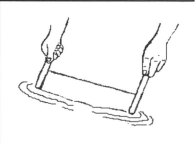

TIP 12

Fly Lines

If by accident you get some gasoline, insect repellent, or a solvent on your line, wash the line ASAP with a mild detergent.

Be especially careful with insect repellent; wash your hands after you apply it, and don't start fishing until you do.

TIP 13

Leader Selection

Always select a tapered leader with a butt section diameter that is close to the diameter of the fly line.

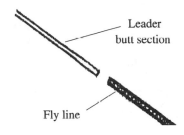

Leader
butt section

Fly line

Gasoline

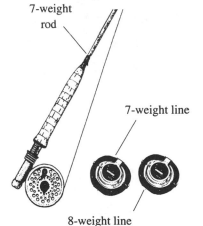

7-weight
rod

7-weight line

8-weight line

TIP 14

Line Weight

Most manufacturers of fly rods list the proper line to use with the rod for the best results. As an example, a 7-weight rod is made to cast a 7-weight line and so forth.

However, to increase your casting distance, use a fly line that is one weight heavier than the recommended fly line weight for your rod.

The increased line weight will overload the rod, causing it to flex more and lose some line speed, but the distance will increase because the rod is working harder.

───── **TIP 15** ─────

Leader Construction Tip

To make your own leaders, try the following formulas:

9-Foot 4X Leader

Inches	18	18	18	18	7	6	5	18

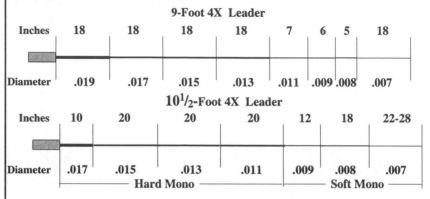

Diameter	.019	.017	.015	.013	.011	.009	.008	.007

10½-Foot 4X Leader

Inches	10	20	20	20	12	18	22-28

Diameter	.017	.015	.013	.011	.009	.008	.007

───── Hard Mono ─────   ───── Soft Mono ─────

───── **TIP 16** ─────

Leader Construction Knot

One of the best knots to use when constructing your own leaders is the blood knot. It's not a difficult knot to tie and is easy to master with a little practice.

STEP 1. Lay the two lines parallel to each other with the ends overlapping by six or eight inches. Grip the two lines at the midpoint with one hand, and begin wrapping the tag end of one of the lines around the other line (at least five turns), bringing the tag end to the midpoint and passing it between both lines.

STEP 2. Changing hands, repeat the procedure with the other tag end while holding the lines at the midpoint.

Step 2

STEP 3. Bring the tag end of the second line and insert it between the lines at the midpoint in the opposite direction of the other line.

Step 1

Step 3

STEP 4. Letting go of the tag end, pull both standing lines in the opposite directions to tighten the knot.

TIP 17
Third Leg

A wading staff can help keep you from
falling into the water when wading in a
river or stream.

The staff serves as a third leg when stepping on
slippery rocks or into deep holes. An easy-to-make staff
is an old ski pole with the basket taken off the bottom of
the pole.

Ski pole

TIP 18
Flotation Vest

When wading new waters for the first time, it's a good
idea to wear a flotation vest. The vest could save your
life.

TIP 19
Homemade Wader Hanger

Here's a simple wader hanger you can make with three coat hangers.
Bend two coat hangers into the shape shown below. Cut out two wire
pieces from the third hanger, and make the hooks as shown below.

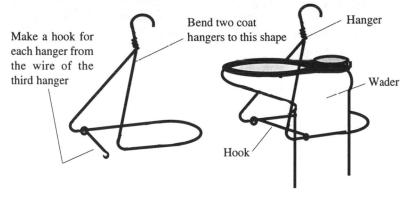

Make a hook for
each hanger from
the wire of the
third hanger

Bend two coat
hangers to this shape

Hanger

Wader

Hook

TIP 20

Wader Repairs

If your waders start to leak while you're fishing, you can use a match or lighter and a plastic worm to make an emergency repair.

Melt the plastic worm with the lighter or match, and use it to seal the hole. Be careful not to burn yourself when you spread the melted plastic.

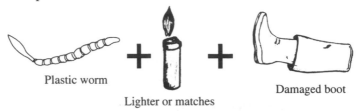

Plastic worm

Lighter or matches

Damaged boot

TIP 21

Wader Care

After using waders, be sure to thoroughly dry them inside and out before storing them for your next trip. A simple way to dry them is to use an electric fan with the airflow directed inside the waders. Most waders will be completely dry in about fifteen minutes.

Another method is to fold down the top of the waders as far as you can and stuff loose crumpled sheets of newspaper into the boot legs. The paper will absorb the moisture in the boots, which then evaporates. If the boots are really wet, you may need to replace the paper a few times.

Drying your waders will prevent mildew and extend their life.

TIP 22

Tail Pickup

If you forget your net or you don't have one, try this trick when landing a salmon.

After the fish is played out, grasp its tail section with your thumb toward the tail.

Don't try to grasp it with your thumb toward the head as your grip won't be as strong, and the tail is more likely to slip out of your hand.

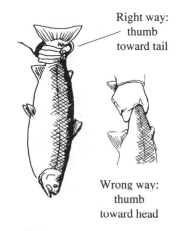

Right way: thumb toward tail

Wrong way: thumb toward head

TIP 23

Changing Patterns

If your eyesight is not what it used to be and you have a difficult time tying on a small fly while on a stream, do it in the comfort of your home before you hit the water.

Pretie your favorite patterns on to a looped tippet the night before and store them in a resealable plastic bag.

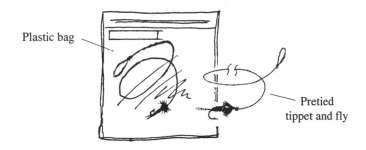

Plastic bag

Pretied tippet and fly

TIP 24

Leader Loop

To make a simple leader loop on your fly line, do the following:

STEP 1. Strip the coating off the last inch of the fly line.
STEP 2. Fray the last $1/8$ inch of the inner core, and form a loop by doubling over the last $1^1/2$ inches of line.
STEP 3. Wrap nylon thread tightly over the core and the last $1/8$ inch of the vinyl coating.
STEP 4. Coat the thread with a pliable waterproof adhesive, and allow it to dry.

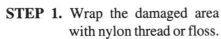

Step 1   Step 2   Step 3   Step 4

TIP 25

Fly Line Repairs

If your fly line gets damaged and hinges, here's a way to repair it so that it still has plenty of life:

Step 1

STEP 1. Wrap the damaged area with nylon thread or floss.
STEP 2. Finish the wrap using a thread loop just as in wrapping a rod guide.

Step 2

STEP 3. Coat the thread over the damaged area with a pliable waterproof adhesive such as Pliobond or Goop.

Step 3

Chapter 8

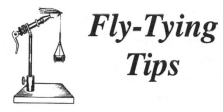 *Fly-Tying Tips*

The following pages contain tips on fly tying. They are only a few of the many tips related to the subject that I have found very useful. Where they came from and who first thought of them may never be answered; however, those tipsters can be proud to know that their ideas are being used.

TIP 1
Health Warning

Many tiers have a habit of moistening materials with their mouths. This is not a safe practice, even if you think the material is clean.

Purchased materials are treated with various chemicals or preservatives, and untreated materials may contain parasites.

Both types can be dangerous to your health if taken internally. Instead use water placed in a small dish that you may access while tying.

H^2O

TIP 2
Purchasing Materials

Materials for ties can be purchased from catalog supply houses, sporting goods stores, or craft shops.

TIP 3
Road Hunting

Road hunting is the act of collecting animals killed by cars or trucks along the road or highway and using the animal fur for ties. If you decide to do it, carry a large plastic garbage bag and a pair of rubber gloves in your car.

TIP 4
Material Sources

Materials for ties can be purchased or obtained from a variety of sources.

Try some of the following: hunters, hunting, chicken farmers, game bird farmers, general farmers, furriers, taxidermists, slaughterhouses, tanneries, garage sales, retail shops, or roadkills.

TIP 5

Storing Furs
and Feathers

Most furs and feathers can be
stored in plastic zippered bags,
plastic boxes with lids, or sealed
glass containers. The containers
should contain a few mothballs
and should be kept in a well-lit
area.

TIP 6

Preventing Infestation

One of the best ways to prevent infestation
is to zap any new fur or feather material in a
microwave oven for a few seconds prior to
storing it with other materials.

TIP 7

Infestation Tip

Turkey and peacock quills and squirrel
tails are prone to moth infestation. Take
exceptional care when adding these materials to your collection.

TIP 8

Storing Necks

Rooster neck

Rooster and hen necks should be stored in un-sealed plastic bags or containers with a few mothballs. Rooster and hen necks contain oils that will migrate into the feathers if they are kept in sealed bags or containers.

TIP 9

Storing Bucktails

Bucktail

Bucktails should also be stored in unsealed plastic bags or plastic containers along with a few mothballs. They also contain oils that will migrate to the hair fibers if the bags or containers are sealed.

TIP 10

Storing
Goose and Duck Quills

When storing duck or goose quills, remove the quills from the wing proper. Also remove the fuzz at the bottom of each feather, and pair up the left and right quills.

─────────────────────────────── **TIP 11** ───────

Dubbing Needle Cleaner

Use an empty film canister to make a container for cleaning your dubbing needle.

Just fill the canister with some medium-weight steel wool, and make a small hole in the center of the cover with a drill or hot nail.

To clean your dubbing needle, poke it through the hole into the steel wool until it comes out clean.

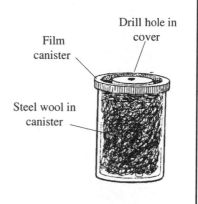

Film canister

Drill hole in cover

Steel wool in canister

TIP 12
Plastic Dubbing Box

Store dubbing in a clear plastic storage box with ¹/₈-inch-diameter holes drilled in the lid over each compartment. **Note:** The hole should be in the center of each compartment.

Fill each compartment with dubbing, and close the lid. Then use your bodkin to pull a little dubbing through each hole in the lid, and you're ready to go.

TIP 13
Storing Dubbing

You can also use a plastic soda straw to store dubbing. A straw cut to a 4-inch length will hold a 3 × 4-inch bag of dubbing. Simply push the dubbing into the straw using a bodkin, crochet needle, or a small-diameter rod.

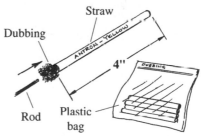

Straw

Dubbing

4"

Rod

Plastic bag

When the straw is full, write the name of the material on the outside of the straw, and store the dubbing straws in a small plastic zippered bag.

TIP 14
Mirror Base

If you don't own a rotary vise, place a mirror under your vise to see the underside of the flies you're tying.

It will help you improve your tying skills to get better results.

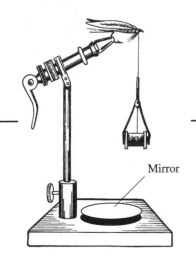

Mirror

TIP 15

Easy Finish

If you can't do a whip finish or you don't know how to use a whip finisher, all you need to finish off a fly, jig, or lure's head is a tube of superglue. Just a dab of glue will do it.

TIP 16

Hook Position

Many tiers secure the hook incorrectly in the vise. Hooks should be placed high and forward with the point exposed, as shown in the illustration.

High and forward with the point exposed

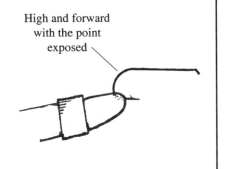

--- **TIP 17** ---

Feather Dusters

A feather duster is a cheap source for hackle or ostrich feathers. Look for the dusters in the houseware aisle of your grocery store. The feathers can be used for tails, streamer wings, and so forth.

Feather duster

TIP 18
Synthetic Dusters

In addition to feather dusters, many grocery stores also carry dusters made of synthetic material that are available in assorted colors. They too are usually found in the houseware aisle and cost very little.

The material comes in about 2- to 3-inch lengths and can be used as a substitute in patterns that call for FisHair or bucktail as wings.

Synthetic duster

--- **TIP 19** ---

Synthetic Furs

As synthetic material becomes more popular as an alternative to real materials, synthetic furs are now available in various colors and lengths and can be purchased in most craft shops. These synthetics can be used for a variety of patterns by creative tiers.

Synthetic fur

TIP 20

Buggy Material

Freezer compartment

To prevent infestation or to alleviate the problem if some of your material becomes infested, try the following.

Place any new or infested material in a zippered plastic bag in the freezer for a few days. The cold will kill any bugs that may be lurking in the material.

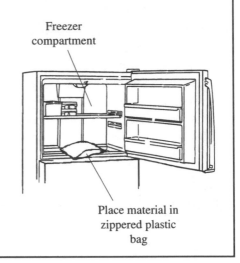

Place material in zippered plastic bag

TIP 21

Trading Material

A great way to grow your collection of tying materials is to trade with other fly tiers or with someone who hunts, especially if you don't.

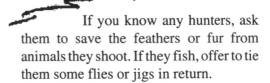

If you know any hunters, ask them to save the feathers or fur from animals they shoot. If they fish, offer to tie them some flies or jigs in return.

TIP 22

Bungee Cord Legs

A great source for rubber legs for your flies is a bungee cord with a braided cloth cover. The cord is composed of thin rubber bands under the cover that can be used as leg material for bass bugs, panfish flies, and nymphs.

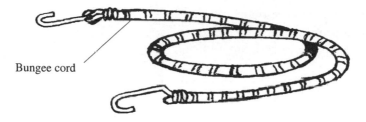

Bungee cord

TIP 23

Tying in Beards

A simple way to tie in a hackle-type beard on any type of pattern is to first snip out a section of the hackle. Then loosely secure the stem under the shank with your thread, and pull the stem back through the thread over the hackle fibers. Secure the fibers with the thread, and snip off the remaining stem to finish the beard.

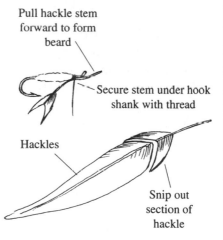

Pull hackle stem forward to form beard

Secure stem under hook shank with thread

Hackles

Snip out section of hackle

TIP 24

Material Storage

An easy way to store your material is to put it in a large zippered storage bag and then attach the bag to a pants hanger with clips.

The hanger can be hung on a rod or rack in your work area.

TIP 25
Tying Table Toolholder

The next time you're in a craft store, buy yourself a styrofoam block approximately $8^1/_2 \times 11 \times 2$ inches thick to use as a toolholder on your tying table.

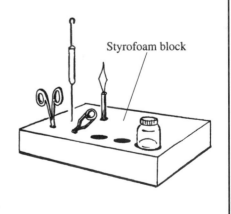

Styrofoam block

When you finish using a tool, jam it into the styrofoam until you need it again. You can even cut some holes in the block to hold your head cement or other items. When the block starts to deteriorate from extended use, replace it with a new one.

Chapter 9

Care, Cleaning, and Cooking Tips

—————— **TIP 1** ——————

Three Basic Ways
to Prepare Fish for Cooking

Method 1

Filleted: Sides of fish are cut off lengthwise along the backbone.

Fillet

Method 2

Dressed or pan-dressed: Fish is scaled, gutted with fins, and its tail is removed.

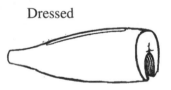

Dressed

Method 3

Steaked: Larger fish is cut into cross-sectional slices.

Steaks

TIP 2

Filleting Panfish

Use this method to fillet smaller fish, such as bluegills, sunfish, rock bass, and crappie.

STEP 1. Using a scraper, scrape off the scales forward toward the head. Then using a knife, cut off the head at an angle behind the gill covers.

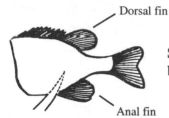

Dorsal fin

Anal fin

STEP 2. Using a fillet knife, cut along both sides of the anal and dorsal fins.

STEP 3. Using pliers, pull out the fins by grasping them at the rear and pulling forward. This should also remove the entrails; however, you may need to use your fingers to remove them.

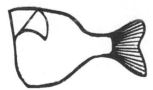

STEP 4. Using the pliers, grasp the skin at the top and peel it off on both sides.

STEP 5. Using the knife, cut off the tail. The fish is now ready for cooking.

———— **TIP 3** ————

Skinning Bullhead

The following method is used to dress out a bullhead or a small catfish.

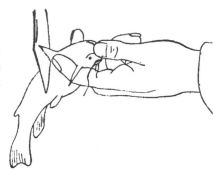

STEP 1. Using a sharp knife, cut directly behind the spinous dorsal fin down to the backbone.

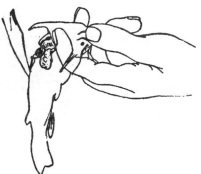

STEP 2. Bend the body sharply down to break the backbone and expose the air bladder and entrails. Then using the knife, slit the skin down the back to the tail.

STEP 3. Grasp the severed backbone with one hand and the head with the other, and pull with each hand in opposite directions. The head, entrails, and skin are removed in one motion, leaving nothing but edible flesh.

TIP 4

Skinning Catfish

The following method is used to dress out a catfish. Keep in mind that a freshly caught fish will skin easier.

STEP 1. Using a sharp knife, cut directly behind the head down to the backbone.

STEP 2. Grasp the skin at the cut with a pair of pliers and pull it toward the tail. One pull on each side of the dorsal fin should tear off the skin on each side.

STEP 3. Bend the body sharply down to break the backbone and expose the air bladder and entrails.
   Then remove the entrails, belly flesh, and front fins along with the head in one motion.

STEP 4. Remove the remaining fins and tail to complete the dressing.

————— **TIP 5** —————

Filleting Pike

The following illustrations show a simple method to fillet a pike and remove those pesky Y bones.

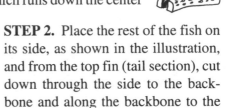

STEP 1. Starting with the top of the fish, cut down behind the head to the backbone. Follow the backbone back to the top rear fin and cut up and remove the piece from the fish, as shown in the illustration. Next, lay the piece on its side and cut it lengthwise along the cartilage, which runs down the center of the piece (both sides).

STEP 2. Place the rest of the fish on its side, as shown in the illustration, and from the top fin (tail section), cut down through the side to the backbone and along the backbone to the tail. Repeat this step on the opposite side.

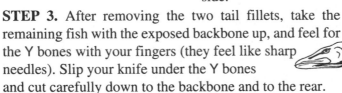

STEP 3. After removing the two tail fillets, take the remaining fish with the exposed backbone up, and feel for the Y bones with your fingers (they feel like sharp needles). Slip your knife under the Y bones and cut carefully down to the backbone and to the rear.

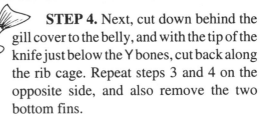

STEP 4. Next, cut down behind the gill cover to the belly, and with the tip of the knife just below the Y bones, cut back along the rib cage. Repeat steps 3 and 4 on the opposite side, and also remove the two bottom fins.

STEP 5. Take all the fillets and remove the skin by inserting the blade between the skin and meat and pulling on the skin while holding the knife in a stationary position.

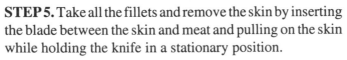

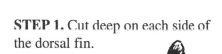

TIP 6

Filleting Bass

The following illustrations show a simple method to fillet largemouth and smallmouth bass.

STEP 1. Cut deep on each side of the dorsal fin.

STEP 2. Cut deep around head, gills, and fins.

STEP 3. Separate the flesh from the rib cage.

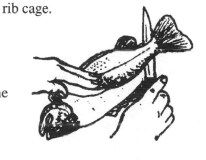

STEP 4. Cut fillet loose from the fish.

STEP 5. Repeat steps 1 through 5 on the opposite side.

STEP 6. Skin fillets by starting at the tail end inserting the blade between skin and meat.

TIP 7

Filleting
Walleye, Sauger, and Perch

Use the following method to fillet walleye, sauger, or jumbo perch.

STEP 1. Insert the knife blade on one side of the dorsal fin all the way through the body and out the belly just behind the vent. Slice along the edge of the anal fin and along the backbone until you reach the tail and cut the fillet loose at the back.

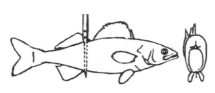

STEP 2. Next, using the knife, slice at an angle from the top of the back behind the head and the pectoral and pelvic fins.

STEP 3. Next, go back to where you started and slice forward along the backbone, dorsal fin, and rib cage toward the head, separating the fillet from the body.

Repeat steps 1 to 3 on the other side.

STEP 4. To remove the skin, lay the fillet skin down, and make a tab between the flesh and the skin with your knife.

Grasp the tab with a pair of pliers and place the knife blade between the flesh and the skin. Pull on the skin while making a seesaw motion with the blade until you remove the skin.

―――――― **TIP 8** ――――――
Dressing Trout

Trout should be dressed as soon as possible after they are caught. Use the following method:

STEP 1. Insert a knife in the vent and slit the belly forward to the V joining the belly to the head.

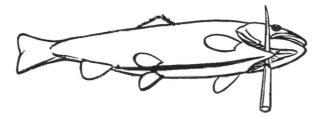

STEP 2. With the knife, cut the V under the throat, and using your fingers, remove the gills and gill rakers from the head.

STEP 3. Next, use your fingers to remove the entrails and the blood streak along the fish's spine. Wash out the body cavity with clean water, and pat it dry with a paper towel. Refrigerate or freeze the fish until you're ready to cook it.

——— **TIP 9** ———

Dressing Salmon

Salmon should be dressed as soon as possible after they are caught. Use the following method:

STEP 1. Insert a knife in the vent and slit the belly forward to the V joining the belly to the head.

STEP 2. With the knife, cut the V under the throat, and using your fingers, remove the gills and gill rakers from the head.

STEP 3. Next, use your fingers to remove the entrails and the blood streak along the fish's spine. Wash out the body cavity with clean water, and pat it dry with a paper towel. Refrigerate or freeze the fish until you're ready to cook it.

Cooking Panfish

The following are a few ways to prepare panfish, fish such as bluegills, sunfish, crappie, rock bass, and so forth. You can use any one of these fish for these recipes, according to your taste or appetite.

Cornmeal Panfish

- 1 to 2 lbs. of panfish fillets
- 1 cup of Crisco oil or bacon grease
- 2 cups of cornmeal

TIP 10

Cooking Instructions

Heat the oil or grease in a skillet or frying pan. Rinse and drain the fillets in cold water, and roll them in the cornmeal. Place the fillets in the pan or skillet, and cook them until golden brown on both sides. Serves 4 to 6.

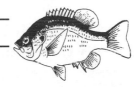

TIP 11

Panfish Bites

- 1 to 2 lbs. of bluegill, sunfish, or crappie fillets
- 2 whole eggs mixed lightly in a bowl with 1 tablespoon of water
- 2 cups of soda crackers crumbed in a blender

Cooking Instructions

Dip the fish fillets in the egg mixture, and roll them in the soda cracker crumbs. Fry on both sides in $1/8$ to $1/4$ inch of cooking oil until they are a golden brown. Salt lightly, and serve hot with cocktail sauce. Serves 4 to 6.

Cooking Panfish

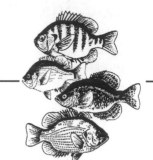

TIP 12

Cooking Instructions

Melt the butter in the pan. Next, dip the fillets in flour, and place them in the butter when it begins to bubble. Add the nuts to the pan, stirring them frequently so they brown but don't burn.

Turn the fillets over once and sprinkle them lightly with salt and pepper. After the fish is done, pour the butter and the almonds over the fillets and serve with a lemon wedge.

Almond Pan-Fried Panfish

- 2 lbs. of panfish fillets
- $1/4$ cup of sliced almonds
- Flour
- Salt and pepper
- $1/4$ lb. of butter

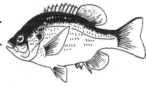

TIP 13

Fried Panfish Chunks

- 2 lbs. of bite-size panfish chunks
- Milk
- Salt and pepper
- 2 eggs
- Beer
- Biscuit mix
- Cornmeal
- $1/4$ lb. butter, margarine, or cooking oil

Cooking Instructions

Soak the chunks in milk, and sprinkle them with salt and pepper. Next, mix together the eggs and beer and dip the fish chunks in the mixture.

Stir together the biscuit mix and the cornmeal. Roll the chunks in the mix, and flash fry them.

Cooking Panfish

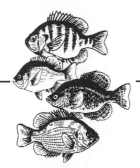

Fried Panfish Fillets

- 1 lb. of panfish fillets
- $^1/_2$ cup of flour
- Salt and pepper
- 1 egg beaten
- 1 cup of Crisco or Puritan oil

TIP 14

Cooking Instructions

Heat the oil or grease in a skillet or frying pan. Rinse and drain the fillets in cold water, and sprinkle them with salt and pepper.

Then dip them in the beaten egg, and roll them in the flour.

Place the fillets in the pan or skillet, and cook them until golden brown on both sides. Serves 4 to 6.

TIP 15

Bluegill Casserole

- 4 cups of bluegill fillets
- $^1/_4$ lb. butter
- 1 cup of milk
- $1^1/_2$ tbsps. of grated onions
- 3 tbsps. Worcestershire sauce
- Dash of pepper
- 1 green pepper
- 4 slices of white bread, crust removed
- 3 tbsps. chopped parsley
- $^3/_4$ tsp. of salt
- Dash of Tabasco sauce

- 1 tsp. of dry mustard
- 1 freshly cut pimento

Cooking Instructions

Drop the fillets in boiling water, bring them to a boil again, and then remove and drain them.

Cook everything together except the fish for 10 minutes. Then add the fish and cook another 5 minutes. Put everything into a casserole dish, and sprinkle with crumbled corn flakes. Brown at 350° for 10 to 15 minutes. Serves 4 to 6.

Cooking Perch

Perch is one of the best-tasting freshwater fish you can eat. Related to the walleye, it is found throughout the midwest and the Great Lakes region of the United States. The following recipes offer unique ways to prepare perch.

— TIP 16 —

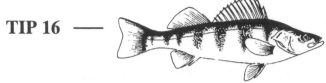

Stir-Fried Perch

- 1 to $1^1/_2$ lbs. of perch fillets
- 1 bunch of shallots
- 1 stalk of broccoli
- 1 pkg. of frozen snow peas or 1 cup of fresh snow peas
- 3 peeled carrots
- 1 can of sliced water chestnuts
- 3 tablespoons of soy sauce
- 2 tablespoons of oil
- $1/_2$ teaspoon of garlic powder
- $1/_4$ teaspoon of white pepper
- 2 tablespoons of water
- 2 tablespoons of cornstarch
- Cooking oil

Cooking Instructions

Cut the fillets into $1^1/_2$-inch squares and marinade them for a half hour in a mixture of 3 tablespoons of soy sauce, 2 tablespoons of oil, $1/_2$ teaspoon garlic powder, and $1/_4$ teaspoon white pepper. Next, chop the broccoli into bite-size pieces. Slice the shallots and carrots diagonally, and drain the water off the chestnuts.

Heat 2 tablespoons of oil in a wok, and fry the fish pieces on both sides until cooked through. Remove them from the wok. Heat 3 more table-spoons of oil in the wok and add the vegetables, stirring occasionally until they are crisp and tender. Add 2 tablespoons of water, 1 teaspoon of soy sauce, and 2 tablespoons of cornstarch to the remaining marinade and stir it in to the vegetable mixture, cooking it for a few more minutes. Add the fish and again heat it for an additional few minutes. Serve on a bed of rice.

Cooking Perch

TIP 17

Cooking Instructions

Perch Parmesan

- 2 lbs. of perch fillets
- 3 cups of cracker crumbs
- 2 eggs
- 1 tsp. of black pepper
- Cooking oil
- Parmesan cheese

Beat eggs and pepper together until well mixed. Dip the fillets into the eggs, and then roll them in cracker crumbs. Heat oil in a pan until hot, and add the fish.

Cook on both sides until golden brown. Salt lightly and sprinkle with Parmesan cheese while the fish is still hot.

TIP 18

Perch with Cheese Sauce

- 2 lbs. of perch fillets
- Salt and pepper
- 4 lean bacon strips
- 1 large onion, sliced

- 2 large tomatoes, thinly sliced
- 1 $1/2$ teaspoons of lemon juice
- 1 can (11 oz.) of cheddar cheese soup or thick cheese sauce

Cooking Instructions

In a well-greased casserole, arrange the ingredients in layers in the following order: bacon strips, sliced onions, sliced tomatoes, and perch fillets seasoned with salt and pepper and lemon juice.

Then cover the fillets with cheddar cheese soup or thick cheese sauce. Bake in a 350° oven for 20 minutes or until the fish flakes off when tested with a fork. Serves 6.

Cooking Salmon

Properly prepared, fresh salmon provide a delicious and unique-tasting meal. Any method of preparation such as grilling, broiling, baking, or steaming will be excellent. The following are a few creative ways to prepare a delicious salmon meal.

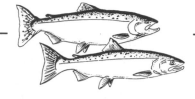

TIP 19

Grilled Salmon

- Salmon steaks or fillets
- Butter
- 1 garlic clove, crushed
- BBQ sauce, hickory-flavored
- Aluminum foil

Cooking Instructions

Place the grill about $3^1/_2$ to 4 inches above the coals. Cover the grill with foil pierced with holes to allow the oils to drain away.

Place the fish on the grill and baste the fillets or steaks with plain butter or butter and garlic or butter and BBQ sauce.

Close the grill and broil the fish for about 10 to 20 minutes, turning the fillets or steaks over and basting them every five minutes.

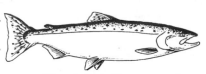

TIP 20

Broiled Salmon Steaks

- 6 1-inch-thick salmon steaks
- $^1/_3$ cup butter
- $^1/_2$ teaspoon salt
- $^1/_4$ teaspoon paprika
- 1 teaspoon Worcestershire sauce
- 6 teaspoons of grated onion

Cooking Instructions

Place the six steaks in a greased shallow baking pan. Melt the butter and add the salt, paprika, and Worcestershire sauce.

Brush the mixture over each salmon steak and then sprinkle with a teaspoon of grated onion.

Place in a preheated oven, and bake for about 25 to 30 minutes.

Cooking Salmon

── TIP 21 ──

Baked Coho

- 2 lbs. of coho salmon fillets
- $1/2$ cup of thick French dressing
- 2 tablespoons of lemon juice
- 1 can ($3^1/_2$ ounces) of French fried onions
- $1/4$ teaspoon of salt
- $1/4$ cup of Parmesan cheese

Cooking Instructions

Preheat oven to 350° F. Cut the fillets into serving-size pieces, and place them in a shallow dish.

Next combine the dressing, lemon juice, and salt, and pour the sauce over the fish. Allow it to stand for 30 minutes.

After 30 minutes, remove the fish from the sauce and place the fillets in a shallow baking pan. Crush the onions and mix them with the Parmesan cheese; sprinkle the mixture over the fish. Bake for 25 to 30 minutes or until the fish flakes easily when tested with a fork. Serves 6.

── TIP 22 ──

Salmon Mishicot-Coho

- 1 pink salmon coho fillet (pour off liquid for sauce)
- $1/2$ cup of melted butter
- 1 cup of milk
- 3 tablespoons of catsup
- 1 cup cracker crumbs

Sauce

- Liquid from salmon fillet
- 2 tablespoons of melted butter
- 1 tablespoon of flour
- $1/2$ cup of milk
- 1 tablespoon of catsup

Cooking Instructions

Mix together butter, milk, and catsup. Coat the salmon in crumbs and place them in a large saucepan on a wire rack about 1 or 2 inches above the bottom. Add 2 cups of water to the pan, cover it, and steam the fillets for 45 minutes.

137

Cooking Trout

If you enjoy eating trout, try the following recipes with steelhead, brown, rainbow, brook, or lake trout.

Foil Grilled Trout

- Fillet steelhead, rainbow, brown, or brook trout
- 1 onion, sliced
- 1 can of peas
- 2 potatoes, sliced
- 1 small can of stewed tomatoes
- Salt and pepper
- Butter
- Lemon juice

TIP 23

Cooking Instructions

Cut fillets into serving-size pieces, and place them on a large piece of doubled foil.

Cover the fish with the vegetables, salt and pepper, butter, and lemon juice.

Fold both ends of the foil together, and cook over the grill for about 40 minutes.

TIP 24

Broiled Lake Trout

- 1 large lake trout
- 1 pressed garlic clove
- 2 tablespoons of olive oil
- $1/4$ teaspoon of white pepper

Cooking Instructions

Cut fillets into serving-size pieces, and rub both sides with the garlic, olive oil, and pepper.

Place the pieces in a shallow pan in a preheated broiler, and broil until browned, turning them once. Spread the fillets with lemon butter, and garnish with thinly sliced lemon and parsley.

Lemon Butter

- $1/4$ lb. of butter
- 1 tablespoon of lemon juice
- 1 teaspoon of grated lemon rind

Cooking Instructions

Melt the butter, and add the lemon juice and rind.

Cooking Walleye and Sauger

Walleye and sauger are excellent-tasting freshwater fish. Enjoy them with the following simple recipes.

TIP 25 —

Crispy Walleye or Sauger

- 6 pan-dressed walleye or sauger fillets
- 1 beaten egg
- 2 tablespoons of milk
- 1 teaspoon salt
- 1 teaspoon chili powder
- 5 or 6 drops liquid hot sauce
- $\frac{1}{2}$ cup cornmeal
- $\frac{1}{2}$ cup flour
- Frying fat
- Hot chili sauce

Cooking Instructions

Combine egg, milk, salt, chili powder, and liquid hot sauce. Dip fish into mixture and roll in cornmeal-flour mix. Place in single layer in hot fat in the frying pan, and fry at moderate heat about 5 minutes on each side. Serve with hot chili sauce. Serves 4 to 6.

— TIP 26 —

Walleye or Sauger Chowder

- 2 lbs. of walleye or sauger fillets cubed
- 4 medium-size potatoes, cubed
- 3 carrots, sliced
- 1 can of drained mushrooms
- 1 pint of half & half
- 1 can of creamed corn

Cooking Instructions

Cook the potatoes and carrots until soft. Drain off the water, saving just enough to cook about 10 minutes more.

Add the fish, mushrooms, half & half, and creamed corn to the water.

Cook for about 10 minutes, adding milk if the chowder is too thick.

139

Cooking Bullhead

Bullhead may be prepared in a wide variety of ways; however, the following are a few recipes worth trying.

TIP 27

Cooking Instructions

Baked Bullhead

- 2 lbs. of skinned bullhead fillets
- 1 cup of sour cream
- $1/2$ cup of chopped green onion tops
- $1/2$ cup of Parmesan cheese
- 2 teaspoons of paprika

Cut the fillets into serving-size portions, and place them in a well-greased baking dish. Place the sour cream, chopped green onion tops, and Parmesan cheese over the fish.

Bake in a 350° oven for 25 to 30 minutes, until the fish flakes when touched with a fork. Remove from the oven and sprinkle with the paprika.

TIP 28
Fried Bullhead

- 3 lbs. of skinned bullhead fillets
- Salt and pepper
- Milk
- Flour
- Butter (5 oz.)
- 2 lemons
- 2 teaspoons of chopped parsley

Cooking Instructions

Season fillets with salt and pepper, dip them in the milk, and roll them in the flour.

Next, melt the butter in a frying pan or skillet. Add the fillets, and cook them on both sides until a nice golden brown.

Place the cooked fillets on a platter and sprinkle them with chopped parsley and the juice of two lemons.

Pour any remaining butter from the pan or skillet over the fish. Serves 6.

Cooking Suckers and Carp

Few fishermen cook or eat suckers or carp; however, the following recipes are worth trying.

TIP 29
Boiled Sucker

- 2 lbs. of dressed sucker
- 1 tablespoon of lemon juice
- $1/2$ cup of chopped celery (leaves and all)
- 1 sliced lemon
- 1 teaspoon of salt

Cooking Instructions

Place the fish in a kettle, and add enough water to cover it. Remove the fish; add the lemon juice, salt, and chopped celery, and bring the water to a boil.

Return the fish to the water, cover the kettle, and lower the heat to a simmer. Cook the fish until tender, and then drain and place it on a platter. Garnish with lemon slices, and serve with melted butter.

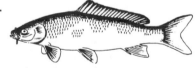

Sweet and Sour Carp

- 2 lbs. of filleted carp
- 1 cup of vinegar
- $1^1/2$ cups of water
- 1 sliced onion
- 1 sliced lemon
- 12 raisins
- 6 whole cloves
- Bay leaf
- Salt
- 1 tablespoon of brown sugar

TIP 30

Cooking Instructions

Place the vinegar, water, onion, lemon, raisins, cloves, and bay leaf in a saucepan and bring to a boil.

Cut the fish fillets crosswise, salt them, and add them to the saucepan.

Reduce the heat, and simmer until the fish is done. Remove the fish, add sugar to the liquid, and bring it to a boil. Pour the boiling sauce over the fish. Chill and serve cold.

Try the following recipes on northern pike or pickerel.

— TIP 31 —

Grilled Pike

- 2 lbs. of pike fillets
- $1/2$ cup of cooking oil
- $1/4$ cup of lemon juice
- 2 teapoons of salt
- $1/2$ teaspoon of Worcestershire sauce
- $1/4$ teaspoon of white pepper
- Dash of Tabasco
- Paprika

Cooking Instructions

Cut the fish into serving-size portions. Combine all the ingredients, except for the paprika and the fish, to make a sauce. Place the fish in a well-greased broiler pan, and baste the fish with the sauce. Sprinkle on the paprika. Cook about 8 minutes; turn the fish and baste, and add the paprika to the other side. Cook for another 7 to 10 minutes.

— TIP 32 —

Baked Pickerel

- 2 lbs. of pickerel fillets
- $1^1/2$ teaspoons of salt
- $1/4$ teaspoon of pepper
- 2 cans of sliced mushrooms
- $1/4$ cup of chopped onions
- 2 tablespoons of cooking oil
- $1/4$ cup of grated cheese
- $1/2$ cup of chopped parsley
- 1 beaten egg
- 1 tablespoon of lemon juice
- $1^1/2$ cups of bread crumbs
- 1 large tomato cut into 6 slices

Cooking Instructions

Cut the fish into serving-size portions, and salt and pepper both sides.

Place in a well-greased baking dish. Cook the mushrooms and onion in the oil until tender. Combine the egg and lemon juice, and brush the mixture onto the fish. Top the fish with bread crumbs and tomato slices.

Sprinkle with salt and pepper, and spread mushroom mixture over tomatoes. Sprinkle with cheese. Bake at 350° for 30 to 40 minutes.

Cooking Bass

The following recipes can be used for largemouth or smallmouth bass.

TIP 33

Sour Cream Baked Bass

- 2 lbs. of skinned bass fillets
- 1 large lime
- $\frac{1}{2}$ pint of sour cream
- Salt
- Pepper

Cooking Instructions

Preheat the oven to 350° degrees. Place the fish in a buttered baking dish. Season the sour cream with salt and pepper and squeeze in the juice from the lime. Grate the rind.

Pour the sour cream over the fish, and sprinkle with the grated rind. Bake in the oven for about 30 minutes or until the fish flakes when tested with a fork.

TIP 34

Onion Soup Baked Bass

- 2 lbs. of bass fillets
- 1 can of cream of onion soup
- 2 tablespoons of chopped onion
- $\frac{3}{4}$ teaspoon of salt
- 1 cup of grated cheese

Cooking Instructions

Cut fillets into serving-size portions, and place them in a greased baking dish. Mix the onion soup, chopped onion, salt, and pepper, and spread the mixture over the fish. Sprinkle the fish with the grated cheese, and bake in a preheated oven at 350° for 25 to 30 minutes or until it flakes easily when tested with a fork.

Cooking Striped, White, and Yellow Bass

Striped, white, and yellow bass can be prepared in a wide variety of ways. Give the following recipes a try.

TIP 35

Baked
White or Yellow Bass

- 2 lbs. of white or yellow bass fillets
- $1/2$ pt. sour cream
- 1 large lime
- Salt and pepper

Cooking Instructions

Arrange the fillets in a buttered baking dish. Squeeze out the juice of the lime and grate the rind. Season the sour cream with salt and pepper and mix in the lime juice. Pour the mixture over the fillets and sprinkle the top with the grated lime rind. Bake in a preheated 350° oven for about 30 minutes or until the fish flakes with a fork. Serves 4.

TIP 36

Wine-Baked Striper

- 4 to 5 lbs. whole cleaned striped bass
- 2 cups of Sauterne
- Salt and pepper

Cooking Instructions

Salt and pepper fish to taste. Place fish in a baking pan, and pour the wine over it. Place the pan in a 350° preheated oven, and cook about 5 minutes per pound on each side.

When done, place on serving platter, and spoon juice over the fish. Serves 4 to 6.

144

Cooking Drum

Few fishermen cook or eat freshwater drum; however, the following recipes are worth trying.

TIP 37

Deep-Fried Drum

- 2 lbs. of drum fillets
- $1/2$ cup of flour
- Salt and pepper
- 1 egg, beaten
- 1 cup of Crisco or vegetable oil

Cooking Instructions

Heat the oil or grease in a skillet or frying pan. Rinse and drain the fillets in cold water, and sprinkle them with salt and pepper.

Dip them in the beaten egg, and roll them in the flour.

Place the fillets in the pan or skillet, and cook them until golden brown on both sides. Serves 4 to 6.

TIP 38

Drum Au Gratin

- 2 lbs. of drum fillets
- 1 tablespoon of melted butter
- $1/2$ lb. of thinly sliced mushrooms
- 2 onions, sliced
- 2 tablepoons of water
- Salt and pepper to taste
- $1/2$ cup of sour cream
- 5 tablespoons of grated cheese
- 1 tablespoon of bread crumbs

Cooking Instructions

Place the fish in a greased baking dish. Sprinkle the fish with melted butter and salt, and bake for 10 minutes. Saute the mushrooms with the onions, adding salt and pepper to taste. Place mushroom mixture over the fish, and pour the sour cream over the top. Sprinkle with cheese and bread crumbs. Bake for an additional 10 minutes or until the fish flakes when tested with a fork. Serves 6.

Cooking Catfish

Catfish may be prepared in a wide variety of ways; however, give these recipes a try.

TIP 39

Fried Catfish

- 3 lbs. of skinned catfish fillets
- Salt and pepper
- Milk
- Flour

- Butter (5 oz.)
- 2 lemons
- 2 teaspoons of chopped parsley

Cooking Instructions

Season fillets with salt and pepper; then dip them in the milk, and roll them in the flour.

Next, melt the butter in a frying pan or skillet. Add the fillets, and cook them on both sides until golden brown.

After they are cooked, place the fillets on a platter, and sprinkle them with the chopped parsley and the juice of the two lemons. Pour any remaining butter in the pan or skillet over the fish. Serves 6.

TIP 40

Dixie Catfish

Cooking Instructions

Brush the inside and outside of the fish with the dressing. Cut the lemon slices in half and put two halves in each body cavity.

- 6 skinned whole catfish
- 12 thin lemon slices
- $1/2$ cup French dressing
- Paprika

Place the fish in a well-greased baking dish with a lemon slice on each side of the fish. Brush the fish with the remaining dressing, and sprinkle on the paprika. Bake at 350° for 25 to 30 minutes or until the fish flakes easily when tested with a fork. Serves 6.

Fish Chowders

Panfish Chowder

- 2 lbs. of panfish cut into 2-inch squares
- 1 cup of chopped onion

TIP 41

- ¹/₄ cup of melted fat
- 3 cups of bite-size potatoes
- 2 cups of boiling water
- 1¹/₂ teaspoons of salt
- Pepper to taste
- 3 cups of milk
- 1 can cream-style corn

Cooking Instructions

Fry the onion until well cooked. Add the potatoes, water, salt, pepper, and the fish. Cover and cook at a slow simmer for 15 to 20 minutes or until the potatoes are done. Add the milk and corn, and heat again until hot.

TIP 42

New England Fish Chowder

- 1 lb. of fish fillets or steaks cut into 1-inch pieces
- 2 tablespoons of chopped bacon or salt pork

- 1 cup of chopped onion
- 2¹/₂ cups of diced potatoes
- 1¹/₂ cups of boiling water
- 1 teaspoon of salt
- Dash of pepper
- 2 cups of milk
- 1 can cream-style corn

Cooking Instructions

Fry the bacon until crisp. Add the onions, and cook them until tender.

Add the potatoes, water, seasonings, and the fish. Cover and cook at a slow simmer for 15 to 20 minutes or until the potatoes are done. Add the milk and corn, and heat again until hot.

Smoking Tips

TIP 43

Smoking Fish

Cut large fish into two-inch sections; slit smaller fish down the middle into two parts. The fish should be thoroughly cleaned and dried but not skinned. Soak the pieces for 5 to 6 hours in a heavy brine solution made of one-part salt to about ten-parts water. Remove the fish from the brine, rinse it, and allow it to air dry until a film (glaze) forms on the surface.

Next, place the fish in the smoking chamber four feet above the fire, and cook them for 10 to 15 minutes. Smother the fire with damp smoking fuel (birch, maple, oak, etc.), and allow the fish to smoke for another 4 to 5 hours.

TIP 44

Additional Flavors

For additional flavor, add some bay leaves, dill, rosemary, or tarragon to the fish prior to putting it in the smoking chamber.

Smoking Temperatures

Use a cooking thermometer to check the temperature of the smoking chamber. The temperature should be 170° to smoke the following fish pieces:

$1/2$-inch-thick pieces = $1^1/_2$ hours
1-inch-thick pieces = $2^1/_2$ hours
$1^1/_2$-inch-thick pieces = $3^1/_2$ hours

During the smoking process, check the fish by prodding them with a fork at the thickest part. They should flake off when done.

Cleaning Tips

TIP 45

Scaling Fish

When scaling small fish, try dipping them for a very brief moment in a pot of boiling water.

The scales should practically fall off when you use the dull side of a knife or scraper. For larger fish, try to scale them underwater using a large pan or a sink filled with plenty of water. This method holds the mess to a minimum and keeps your hands from having that slimy fish feeling.

TIP 46

SALT

Slippery/Slimy Fish

To remove slime from a fish before cleaning it, dip the fish into a solution of water and a cup full of salt. You can also use salt on your hands during the cleaning process to make the fish less slippery.

TIP 47

Cleaning Small Northerns

To get rid of the Y bones in small northern pike, try the following: Scale, clean, and fillet the fish. Cut out the ribs, and then cut through the skin every $1/4$ inch to the tail section until you don't feel any more Y bones.

Fry the fillet with the cut side to the fire until done, and then flip it over to brown the skin side. This method will dissolve the pesky Y bones during the cooking process and give you a delicious boneless fillet.

Cleaning Tips

TIP 48

Scaling Fish

To prevent a mess when scaling fish indoors, scale them underwater to keep the scales from flying. I use the kitchen or laundry sink and, when done, wash the scales down the drain.

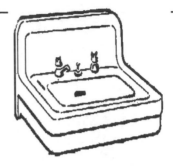

Fresh Fish

For better-tasting fish, clean them as soon as possible after you catch them. They also taste better if you cook them right after you clean them.

TIP 49

TIP 50

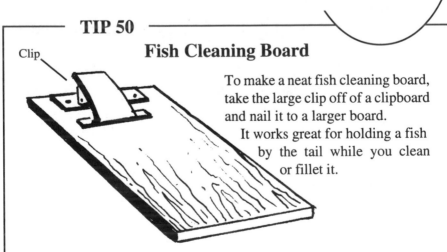

Clip

Fish Cleaning Board

To make a neat fish cleaning board, take the large clip off of a clipboard and nail it to a larger board.

It works great for holding a fish by the tail while you clean or fillet it.

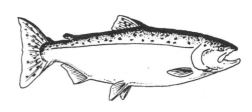

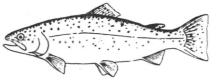

Chapter 10

Fishing Tips by Species

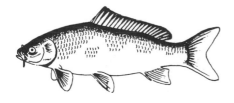

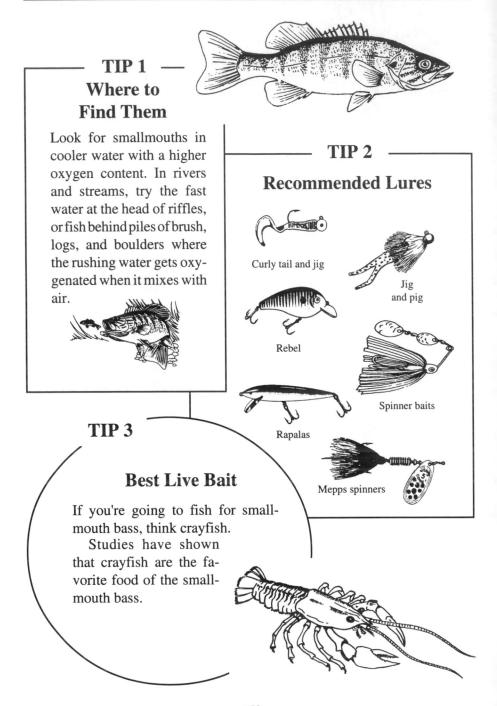

TIP 1 — Where to Find Them

Look for smallmouths in cooler water with a higher oxygen content. In rivers and streams, try the fast water at the head of riffles, or fish behind piles of brush, logs, and boulders where the rushing water gets oxygenated when it mixes with air.

TIP 2

Recommended Lures

Curly tail and jig

Jig and pig

Rebel

Spinner baits

Rapalas

Mepps spinners

TIP 3

Best Live Bait

If you're going to fish for smallmouth bass, think crayfish.
   Studies have shown that crayfish are the favorite food of the smallmouth bass.

── TIP 4 ──
Spring Fishing

Smallmouth are active and spawn in the spring when the water temperature reaches 60 to 65 degrees. The females move to the spawning flats when the water reaches 48 to 54 degrees. Spawning flats are usually gravel flats in 8 to 10 feet of water. Smallmouth often hold at the first deep drop-off at the end of these flats. Try smaller lures and baits during the spring months.

Summer Fishing　　　TIP 5

During the summer months in the south, smallmouth move into water as deep as 50 feet during the daylight hours. At night or in the evening, they move to the shallows, such as humps, points, and sloping banks. In the north, they can be found suspended in the 20-foot zone around reefs, rock piles, and riprap.

Morning or evening is the best time of day to try fishing.

TIP 6
Fall Fishing

Smallmouth move into deeper water in the fall months and can be found suspended over rock banks in 15 to 30 feet of water. They feed mostly at night in shallower water.

── TIP 7 ──

Winter Fishing

During the winter months, smallmouth are the least active and move into deeper water. They can be found suspended over rock banks and bluffs in 8 to 20 feet of water. They feed mostly on schools of baitfish, which they follow into deeper waters where they suspend to depths of 50 feet.

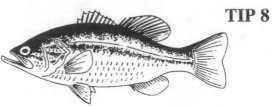

TIP 8

Where to Find Them

If fishing for largemouth bass, always investigate areas where aquatic plants, such as hydrilla, milfoil, eelgrass, coontail, and lily pads are present. In addition to weed beds, largemouths also prefer areas with cover, such as stumps, logs, standing timber, and brush.

TIP 9

Best Lures

By far, plastic worms are the most productive lures to use for largemouth bass. They are among the deadliest of all artificial lures.

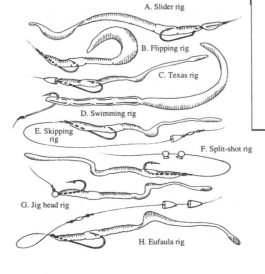

A. Slider rig
B. Flipping rig
C. Texas rig
D. Swimming rig
E. Skipping rig
F. Split-shot rig
G. Jig head rig
H. Eufaula rig

TIP 10

Live Bait Rig

Try the following live bait rig to catch largemouth bass.

Hook a frog through the lips, and attach a slip sinker about 12 inches above the hook with a removable split shot as a stop for the slip sinker.

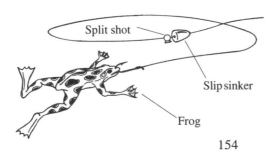

Split shot

Slip sinker

Frog

TIP 11

Spring Fishing

Largemouths spawn in the spring when the water temperature reaches 62 to 65 degrees. The females move to the spawning flats where the males build their nests. Spawning flats are usually gravel flats in 12 to 36 inches of water. The male chases away the female after they spawn and guards the nest until the eggs hatch. Try smaller lures and baits during the spring months.

TIP 12

Summer Fishing

During the summer months when the water temperature reaches 75 degrees or more, largemouths are the most active and can be found in heavy weed cover. They prefer lily pads or heavy patches of aquatic cabbage and can also be found around piers, docks, or bridges. Morning or evening is the best time of day to try fishing.

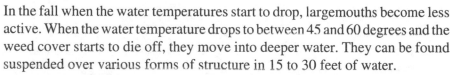

TIP 13

Fall Fishing

In the fall when the water temperatures start to drop, largemouths become less active. When the water temperature drops to between 45 and 60 degrees and the weed cover starts to die off, they move into deeper water. They can be found suspended over various forms of structure in 15 to 30 feet of water.

TIP 14

Winter Fishing

In the northern states, largemouths are the least active during the winter months. They can be found suspended over various forms of structure in 8 to 20 feet of water. They feed mostly on baitfish, which they follow into deeper waters. Try fishing areas where you find aquatic cabbage plants. In the southern states, largemouths are also less active in the winter; however, the same tactics used during the spring season can produce good results.

TIP 15
Where to
Find Them

Most hybrid striped bass are found in large lakes and impoundments throughout the United States. Look for stripers in cooler deep water with a sand or gravel bottom.

Trolling live baits and artificial lures or still fishing are the most effective methods to use. Also watch for birds feeding on the surface—a sure sign of stripers feeding on baitfish near the surface.

TIP 16
Best Live Bait

Shad are one of the best live baits to use for stripers. However, many inland lakes are void of the species, and few bait shops carry them. Large minnows, shiners, chubs, frozen smelt, or alewives also work well, and one type or other can be found in most bait shops.

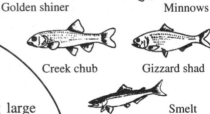

Alewife

Golden shiner

Minnows

Creek chub

Gizzard shad

Smelt

TIP 17
Best Lures

Stripers can be caught using large lures, spoons, spinners, and streamer flies that represent baitfish. Trolling deep water with typical striper trolling rigs like the one shown below is very effective.

TIP 18

Spring Fishing

Striped bass spawn in the spring when the water temperature reaches 55 to 67 degrees. The spawning usually takes place in rocky areas in lakes or rivers and streams with rocky bottoms. Trolling striper rigs near or over spawning areas or using a jig dressed with a baitfish worked deep can produce results during the spring months.

TIP 19

Summer Fishing

During the summer months when the water temperature reaches 72 degrees, stripers are the most active and can be found near the surface feeding on baitfish. Morning or evening is the best time of day to try trolling or casting spoons, spinners, and crankbaits.

TIP 20
Fall Fishing

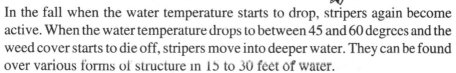

In the fall when the water temperature starts to drop, stripers again become active. When the water temperature drops to between 45 and 60 degrees and the weed cover starts to die off, stripers move into deeper water. They can be found over various forms of structure in 15 to 30 feet of water.

TIP 21

Winter Fishing

In the southern and western states, stripers are the least active during the winter months. They can be found suspended over various forms of structure in deep water.

Try the same tactics used during the spring season to produce good results. Stripers feed mostly on baitfish such as shad or large minnows. Try deep-water trolling or using a jig fished deep.

TIP 22
How to
Find Them

To locate white or yellow bass in a lake, try drift fishing a baited jig in 7- to 15-foot depths just off the bottom.

Also try casting lures or spinners along riprap shorelines.

In rivers or streams, try tailwaters or below dams or rocky areas.

TIP 23
Best Live Bait

Both white and yellow bass prefer minnows or other baitfish. Crayfish, worms, or insect larvae also work well as live bait.

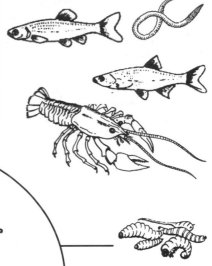

TIP 24
Best Lures

White and yellow bass can be caught by using small spinners, streamer flies, and jigs that represent baitfish. Try casting to riprap or other forms of structure. Also try deep-water jigging.

TIP 25

Spring Fishing

White and yellow bass spawn during the months of March and April when the water temperature reaches 55 to 67 degrees. The spawning usually takes place in lake inlets or rivers and streams with rocky bottoms.

In lakes and rivers, white and yellow bass can be found where food is abundant. Try fishing points at the edge of a channel or in the narrows of the river or stream.

TIP 26

 # Summer Fishing

During the summer months of May through August when the water temperature reaches 76 degrees, white and yellow bass are the most active and can be found near the surface feeding on baitfish. Morning or evening is the best time of day to try trolling or jig fishing with artificial or live baits.

 ## TIP 27
Fall Fishing

In the fall when the water temperature starts to drop, white and yellow bass again become active. When the water temperature drops to between 45 and 60 degrees and the weed cover starts to die off, they move into deeper water. They can be found over various forms of structure in 15 to 30 feet of water.

TIP 28
Winter Fishing

During the winter months, white and yellow bass are the least active. They can be found suspended over various forms of structure in deep water.

However, ice fishermen catch both species in holes 15 or more feet deep by fishing with minnows a few feet off the bottom. In areas without ice, the same tactics used during the spring season can produce good results.

TIP 29
Best Water Temperature and Feeding Mood

Catfish feed most actively when the water temperature is between 65 and 85 degrees.

The best temperature to catch catfish is 75 to 80 degrees, when a catfish's metabolic rate is increased to its maximum. Channel cats prefer moving water, while flatheads stay where the water is quiet.

To get catfish in a feeding mood, fill a quart-size milk carton with chicken or beef liver blood, and punch some holes in the carton. Suspend it over a good catfish hole, and wait about 15 minutes before fishing. Fish a few feet from the carton for the best results.

TIP 30
Time of Day

To improve your ability to catch catfish, try fishing just before daybreak or from dusk to midnight or later.

TIP 31
Equipment/Bait

 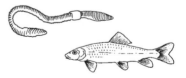

Standard equipment for catfishing consists of a pole with plenty of backbone, 15- to 25-pound test line, and a single 2 or 4 hook tied to a 3- to 6-foot leader attached to a barrel swivel with a sliding sinker above it.

The hook can be baited with any number of concoctions, such as blood baits, stink baits, leeches, worms, chicken entrails, hot dogs, or small fish like bluegills, shad, chubs, or suckers.

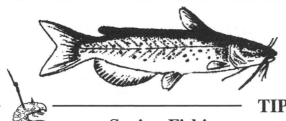

TIP 32
Spring Fishing

Most catfish spawn in the spring or early summer when the water temperature reaches 70 to 75 degrees. The eggs are deposited in a nest built in undercut stream banks or under logs or rocky areas.

Try using small live baits such as crayfish or bluegills. You can also try wax worms or small pieces of hot dog.

TIP 33
Summer Fishing

During the summer months of May through August when the water temperature reaches 76 to 80 degrees, catfish are the most active. Try night fishing, using small bluegills as bait, for the best results.

TIP 34
Fall Fishing

In the fall when the water temperature starts to drop, catfish again become very active.

When the water temperature drops to between 45 and 60 degrees, try still fishing on the bottom from dusk to midnight and again around dawn.

TIP 35

Winter Fishing

During the winter months, catfish are the least active. When the water temperature dips below 40 degrees feeding drops off rapidly. While some species of catfish can be caught ice fishing, you're better off fishing for other species such as panfish or pike during the winter months.

TIP 36

Time of Year/Day

Bullheads probably are caught by more neophyte anglers than any other species of fish. Almost anyone can find bullheads in ponds, rivers, streams, or lakes within a short distance from their home.

Bullheads prefer sluggish waters with weedy bottoms and are cover-oriented. They like rocks, sunken logs, and brush piles.

Bullheads are active from May through October with the peak fishing season from July through September. They are active during evening hours when they feed primarily on insects.

TIP 37

Lima Beans

Here's a tip I got from a young boy fishing at a local pond: If you want to catch bullheads, use lima beans! Bullheads seem to love canned lima beans better than worms or most other baits. At least they do in our local pond.

TIP 38

Equipment/Bait

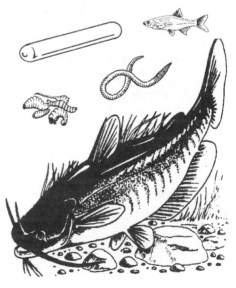

Medium-action equipment rigged with 6- to 8-pound test line and a 6 hook works the best. Sinkers (such as a few split shots) can be used for stream or river fishing; don't use any when fishing lakes or ponds.

The hooks can be baited with lima beans, night crawlers, leaf worms, small minnows, or hot dogs.

TIP 39
Spring Fishing

Most bullheads spawn in the spring or early summer when the water temperature reaches 70 to 75 degrees. The eggs are deposited in a nest built as a depression or in an undercut stream bank or under logs or rocky areas. Try using small live bait, such as worms, wax worms, or small pieces of hot dog, during the warmest part of the day.

TIP 40
Summer Fishing

During the summer months of May through August when the water temperature reaches 78 degrees or more, bullheads are the most active. Almost any bait will produce good results when fished on the bottom.

TIP 41
Fall Fishing

In the fall when the water temperature starts to drop, bullheads again are very active.

When the water temperature drops to between 45 and 60 degrees, try still fishing on the bottom using worms, hot dogs, or wax worms.

TIP 42
Winter Fishing

During the winter months, bullheads are the least active. When the water temperature dips below 40 degrees, feeding drops off rapidly, and they become dormant. During this period, they are very difficult to catch, and you would be better off fishing for other species, such as panfish or pike.

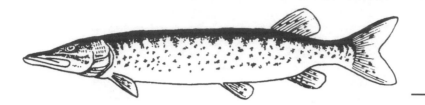

TIP 43
Where to Find Them

Larger muskie are often caught in water greater than 10 feet deep. They migrate to shallower water in search of food and can be found in weedy areas or submerged debris near shore. Casting large bait or lures around logs or weed beds can produce good results.

TIP 44
Live Bait

The best live bait for muskie are suckers, frogs, perch, and large chubs.

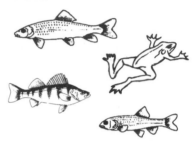

TIP 45
Lures

The most productive lures for muskie are large surface or diving plugs, large spoons, or large bucktail spinners.

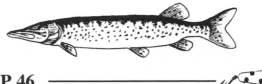

TIP 46
Spring Fishing

In the spring, muskies are sluggish in cold water and preoccupied with spawning. When the water temperature is below 68 degrees in early spring, feeding is slow, making it difficult to entice them to bite. When the water reaches 68 degrees in late spring, they are the most active.

In early spring, cast for muskies using smaller lures or live bait fished in shallows with submerged weed beds. Try using a variety of lures and bait a little smaller than the ones you would use in the summer. In late spring, increase the lure and bait sizes, and fish the weed lines, flats, points, creek mouths, and drop-offs.

TIP 47   Summer Fishing

In the summer months when the water temperature reaches 90 degrees, muskies stop feeding. As the water temperature goes up, the larger muskies move to deeper waters with submerged weed beds or other forms of structure.

During this period, try deep-water trolling to catch summer muskies. Most fish will be found below the 10-foot depth mark and as deep as 30 feet. Try using large deep-water lures, spoons, or bucktails along the edges of weed beds, drop-offs, points, islands, and humps.

TIP 48
Fall and Winter Fishing

In the fall months as the water temperature starts to drop, muskies again become active. They move into the shallows as they did in the spring in search of their next meal.

Casting lures or fishing with live baits in shallow water with submerged weed beds or other forms of structure can produce the best results. Try using a variety of lures and bait fished along weed lines, flats, points, creek mouths, and drop-offs.

In the winter months, muskies move back into deeper water. When the water temperature drops below 68 degrees, feeding slows. In most states, the muskie season is closed to fishing in the winter.

TIP 49
Where to Find Them

Northern pike are found in most lakes and rivers in the northern parts of the United States and in Canada.

They prefer weedy areas with an escape route to deep water.

The most productive time to fish for them is in the spring, using natural live bait or artificial lures resembling baitfish.

TIP 50
Live Bait

Some of the better live baits for large northerns are shiners, tadpoles, frogs, and large chubs.

TIP 51
Lures

The most productive lures for pike are large spoons, noisy surface or diving lures, or large bucktail spinners.

— TIP 52 —

Spring Fishing

Northern pike spawn in the early spring as soon as the ice melts in their spawning areas. Spawning takes place in the weedy shallows as early as March to as late as July in Alaska. Northerns are most active when the water temperature reaches 55 degrees. Fish the weed lines, flats, points, creek mouths, and drop-offs using spoons, spinners, plugs, or live bait.

TIP 53

Summer Fishing

As the water temperature starts to go up during the summer months, northern pike move to deeper waters with submerged weed beds or other forms of structure.

During this period, deep-water trolling is the best way to catch summer northerns. Most fish will be found below the 10-foot depth mark. Try using large deep-water lures, spoons, or bucktails along the edges of weed beds, drop-offs, points, islands, and humps. Also try live bait such as sucker, large golden roaches, or frogs.

TIP 54

Fall Fishing

In the fall when the water temperature starts to drop, northern pike again become active. They move back into the weedy shallows, rocky bars, brush piles, or below rapids or riffles in rivers or streams.

Again, as in the spring, try using spoons, spinners, plugs, or live bait.

TIP 55

Winter Fishing

In the winter months, northerns move into deep water. Try ice fishing using tip-ups baited with shiner minnows or chubs in water over 10 feet deep with submerged weeds.

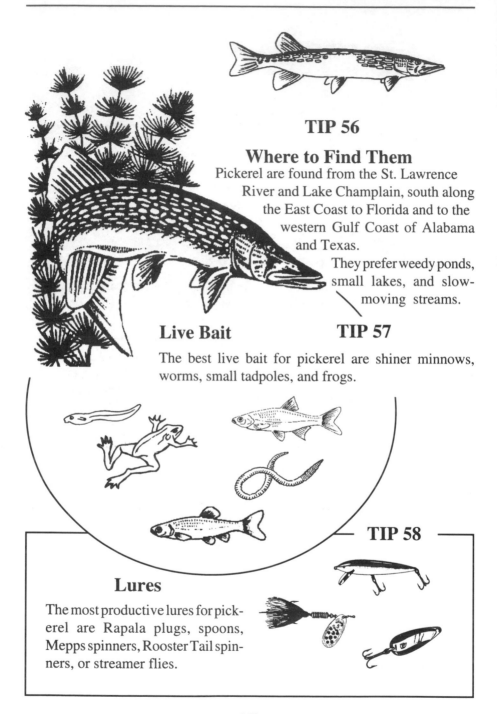

TIP 56

Where to Find Them

Pickerel are found from the St. Lawrence River and Lake Champlain, south along the East Coast to Florida and to the western Gulf Coast of Alabama and Texas.

They prefer weedy ponds, small lakes, and slow-moving streams.

Live Bait   TIP 57

The best live bait for pickerel are shiner minnows, worms, small tadpoles, and frogs.

TIP 58

Lures

The most productive lures for pickerel are Rapala plugs, spoons, Mepps spinners, Rooster Tail spinners, or streamer flies.

TIP 59
Spring Fishing

Pickerel, the smallest member of the pike family, spawn in the early spring about the same time as the pike and musky, just after the ice melts in their spawning areas. Spawning takes place in the weedy shallows from March through May. Like the northern, pickerel are most active when the water temperature reaches 55 to 70 degrees, depending on which part of the country you're in. Fish the weed lines, flats, points, creek mouths, and drop-offs using small spoons, spinners, plugs, or live bait.

TIP 60
Summer Fishing

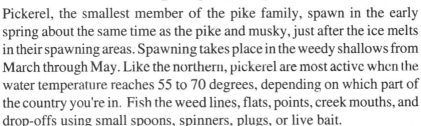

When the water temperature goes up during the summer months, pickerel are able to tolerate the warmer water because of their smaller size and spend most of their time in the weed cover.

During this period, try working the weed beds with a fly rod or spinning outfit using small lures, spoons, spinners, or streamer flies along the edges and pockets of the weed beds. Also try live bait such as minnows, shiners, worms, tadpoles, or frogs.

TIP 61
Fall Fishing

In the fall when the water temperature starts to drop both in the south and north, pickerel become very active. As you did in the spring and summer, use a fly rod or a spinning outfit working the weed beds in the early morning or evening. Try using streamer patterns that imitate baitfish, small spoons, spinners, plugs, or live bait.

TIP 62
Winter Fishing

In the winter months, try ice fishing up north. More pickerel are caught through the ice than during the summer. Use a tip-up baited with a minnow or shiner. In the south, fish the same as you would in the fall.

Panfish

Panfish, the most popular fish in America, are the fish most frequently caught by anglers. Panfish are simply any species of fish small enough to fit into a frying pan. As many as twenty-three various species qualify as panfish, including the following more popular species: yellow, brown, and black bullheads; yellow bass, white bass and white perch; green, orangespotted, spotted, yellowbreast, redear, longear, and pumpkinseed sunfish; white and black crappie; and yellow perch.

── TIP 63 ──

Equipment

The key to enjoyable panfishing is to match your equipment to the conditions and size of the fish you seek. Rod and reel selections usually consist of ultra-light gear, from short delicate rods 4 feet in length to 20-foot noodle rods, matched with tiny reels and equipped with light line in the 2- to 6-pound test class.

TIP 64

Hook Selection

When selecting hooks for panfish with small mouths such as bluegills or pumpkinseeds, use fine wire hooks no larger than an 8 or 10. For panfish with larger mouths, such as white bass, crappie, perch, or rock bass, use a 1 or 2 flexible wire hook.

── TIP 65 ──

Live Bait Selection

For panfish with small mouths, such as bluegills or pumpkinseeds, use smaller bait such as grubs, mousies, maggots, and wigglers. For panfish with larger mouths, such as white bass, crappie, perch, or rock bass, minnows and worms are the preferred bait.

Wigglers

Grubs, mousies, maggots

Small minnows

TIP 66

 ### Spring Fishing

During the spring months, panfish are the most active and provide excellent fishing throughout the United States. They will be found in various types of spawning areas located in the shallows, building a nest and preparing to spawn. At this time of the season, try using light gear and small lures or baits for the best results.

TIP 67
Summer Fishing

In the summer months, most of the larger panfish move out of the shallows to deeper water. They are still active in the early morning or early evening hours. Try using a spinning outfit rigged with a casting bubble with a pair of small jigs and Twister Tails tied in tandem for the best results. Also try live bait or a fly-fishing outfit in the morning or evening.

TIP 68
Fall Fishing

During the fall months, most panfish move back into the shallows. They are still active in the early morning or early evening hours. Try fishing for them the same way you would during the spring months. You can also try the casting-bubble method or a fly rod.

TIP 69
Winter Fishing

In the winter months, try ice fishing up north. More panfish are caught through the ice than any other types of fish. Use a tip-up or a pole baited with a minnow, shiner, wax worm, or grub. Also try jigging with ice spoons or small lures. In the south, try fishing the same as you would in the spring or fall.

TIP 71

Lures

The most productive lures for blue-gills are small jigs dressed with Twister Tails, ice spoons, small spinners, wet flies, nymph patterns, small stream-ers, and insect patterns.

TIP 70

Where to Find Them

Most fishermen pursue the blue-gill more than any other fish. It's the kind of fish that all anglers can catch regardless of age, experience, or type of equipment they own.

Bluegills can be found in rivers, streams, ponds, lakes, and lagoons throughout the United States.

During the spring, look for them in the sun-warmed shallows, making saucer-size impressions in the sandy bottom for spawning.

After spawning, sometime in early summer, they move to deep waters and remain there through most of the summer, fall, and winter months.

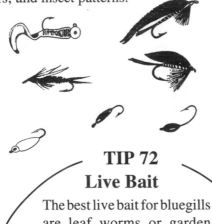

TIP 72
Live Bait

The best live bait for bluegills are leaf worms or garden worms, grubs, wax worms, crickets, grasshoppers, and maggots.

TIP 73
Spring Fishing

In the spring months, bluegills are in their spawning cycle and are the most active. Spawning takes place in late spring or early summer depending on the location. Bluegills will be found in the shallows, building a nest and preparing to spawn. At this time of the season, try using light spinning gear or try fly fishing using small wet flies, lures, or bait.

TIP 74
Summer Fishing

In the summer months, most of the larger bluegills move out of the shallows to deeper water. They are still active in the early morning or early evening hours. Try using a spinning outfit rigged with a casting bubble with a pair of small jigs and Twister Tails tied in tandem, or try live bait or a fly-fishing outfit in the morning or evening.

TIP 75
Fall Fishing

During the fall months, as in the summer months, bluegills remain in the deeper waters. They are still active in the early morning or early evening hours in the shallows. Try fishing for them the same way you would during the spring months. You can also try the casting-bubble method or a fly rod.

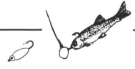

TIP 76
 ### Winter Fishing

In the winter months, try ice fishing up north. Use a tip-up or a pole baited with wax worms or grubs. Also try jigging with ice spoons or small lures. In the south, try fishing the same as you would in the spring or fall.

────── TIP 77 ──────

Where to Find Them

During the spring months of March and April, crappies are the most active and provide excellent fishing when using small jigs or minnows. In early March, they will be found in deeper water around brush piles, rocks, or some type of structure. In late March or early April, they will be spawning in the shallows. During the summer months, they will move back into deep water and stay there until the fall when they again will become more active. When winter sets in, they return to deep water and provide excellent ice fishing opportunities.

TIP 78

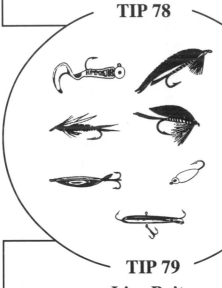

Lures

The most productive lures for crappie are small jigs dressed with Twister Tails, ice spoons, small spinners, wet flies, nymph patterns, small streamers, and insect patterns.

TIP 79

Live Bait

The best live bait for crappie are minnows, wax worms, grubs, or maggots.

TIP 80
Spring Fishing

As water temperatures increase, crappie begin to gather along secondary breaks (cover 10 to 15 feet deep) close to their shallow-water spawning beds. Once you locate their beds, work the deeper waters first, using ultralight equipment and smaller bait or a combination of both artificials and naturals.

TIP 81
Shallow-Water Rig

To make this rig, simply add a float or bobber at the desired depth you want the jig to be (depth can be varied).

You can use a plain jig, or you can dress it with a small minnow. The rig is then cast around weed beds and brush piles, using a slow retrieve and twitching the rod tip as you reel in.

Water line

TIP 82
Jig Fishing

One of the key factors for successful crappie fishing is to use a light line (2- to 6-pound test) and small jigs ($\frac{1}{3}$ to $\frac{1}{8}$ ounce). When using jigs, try different colors and different types. Add Twister Tails or tubes to the jig or use hair/marabou-type jigs.

Cast the jigs and bounce them along the bottom, swim them, or just plain jig them.

You can also try the shallow-water setup if the fish don't want plain jigs.

Float or bobber set at desired depth

6 to 30 inches

Jig

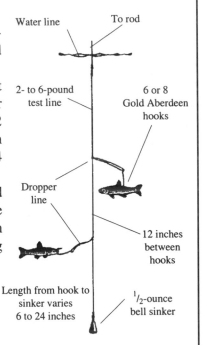

TIP 83

Summer/Fall Fishing

Unlike spring crappie fishing, large crappies can be taken in the summer and fall by fishing waters 25 to 35 feet deep.

Use larger bait, and get it down on the bottom. At this time of the year, crappies will be hugging the bottom in deep water.

TIP 84

Deep-Water Fishing

Deep-Water Rig

With this setup, remove the jig and replace it with a couple of hooks baited with small minnows.

The rig consists of 2- to 4-pound test line with a $^1/_2$-ounce bell or dipsy sinker tied to the end with two dropper lines 12 feet apart. Use lightweight hooks, such as 6 or 8 Gold Aberdeen, tied 12 to 24 inches above the sinker (see diagram).

The distance between the hooks should stay constant at 12 inches; however, the distance from the sinker to the hook can vary from 18 to 24 inches when fishing in heavy brush.

Water line   To rod

2- to 6-pound test line

6 or 8 Gold Aberdeen hooks

Dropper line

12 inches between hooks

Length from hook to sinker varies 6 to 24 inches

$^1/_2$-ounce bell sinker

TIP 85

Winter Crappie Fishing

During the winter months, December through February in the north, crappies will be found in water depths to 30 feet. In the deep water, they will be suspended over rock piles, brush piles, or submerged timbers. Use a deep-water rig baited with small minnows.

In the south, fish crappies in the winter the same way you do in the summer or fall. In the north, try ice fishing with a tip-up or a pole.

TIP 86

Basic Crappie Fishing Rig

The following are a few examples of how to rig your equipment for crappie fishing during the winter season.

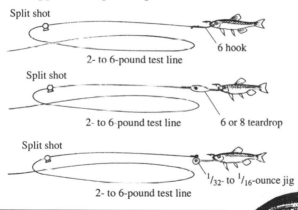

Split shot

6 hook

2- to 6-pound test line

Split shot

6 or 8 teardrop

2- to 6-pound test line

Split shot

$^1/_{32}$- to $^1/_{16}$-ounce jig

2- to 6-pound test line

TIP 87

Jigging Tip

When jig fishing, try different colors such as chartreuse, white, yellow, and purple. If you're not having any luck with one color, switch to another color until you find the right one. Cast the jigs and bounce them along the bottom, swim them, or just plain jig them in both deep and shallow water.

TIP 88
Where to Find Them

Like the bluegill, the rock bass can be found in rivers, streams, ponds, lakes, and lagoons throughout the eastern United States and the upper Mississippi Valley.

During the late spring, look for them in the sun-warmed shallows, making saucer-size impressions in the sandy bottom for spawning. When they finish spawning, they move to areas with a rocky or gravel bottom and remain there through most of the summer.

When the water starts to cool in the fall, they move to deep water and stay there during the winter months.

TIP 89
Equipment/Lures

Rock bass can be caught using basic spinning equipment or by fly fishing. The most productive lures to use for rock bass are small jigs dressed with Twister Tails, ice spoons, small spinners, wet flies, nymph patterns, small streamers, and insect patterns.

TIP 90
Live Bait

The best live bait for rock bass are leaf worms or garden worms, grubs, maggots, wax worms, crickets, grasshoppers, and crayfish.

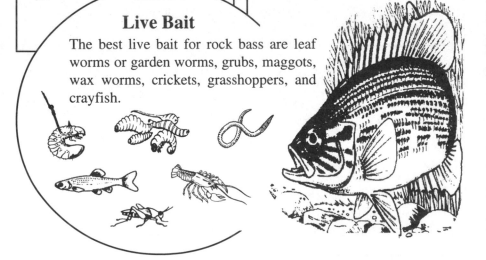

TIP 91

Spring Fishing

In the spring months, rock bass are the most active during their spawning cycle. Spawning takes place in late spring or early summer depending on the location. They will be found in the shallows, building a nest and preparing to spawn. At this time of the season, try light spinning gear or fly fishing using small wet flies, lures, or bait.

TIP 92

Summer Fishing

In the summer months, most rock bass move to areas with rocky or gravel bottoms. They are active during most of the daylight hours. Try using a spinning outfit rigged with a casting bubble with a pair of small jigs and Twister Tails tied in tandem, or try live bait or a fly-fishing outfit in the morning or evening.

TIP 93

Fall Fishing

During the fall months, rock bass move into deeper water.
　　　　They are still active in the early morning or early evening hours in the shallows. Try fishing for them the same way you would during the spring months. You can also try the casting-bubble method.

TIP 94

Winter Fishing

In the winter months, try ice fishing up north. Use a tip-up or a pole baited with wax worms or grubs. Also try jigging with ice spoons or small lures. In the south, try fishing the same as you would in the spring or fall.

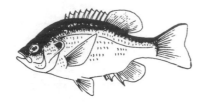

TIP 96

Lures

The most productive lures for sunfish are small jigs dressed with Twister Tails, ice spoons, small spinners, wet flies, nymph patterns, small streamers, and insect patterns.

TIP 95

Where to Find Them

Like the bluegill, the sunfish is a fish that all anglers can catch regardless of their age, experience, or type of equipment they own. Sunfish can be found in rivers, streams, ponds, lakes, and lagoons throughout the United States.

During the spring, look for them in the sun-warmed shallows, making saucer-size impressions in the sandy bottom for spawning. When they finish spawning, sometime in early summer, they move to deep waters and remain there through most of the summer, fall, and winter months.

TIP 97

Live Bait

The best live bait for sunfish are leaf worms or garden worms, grubs, wax worms, crickets, grasshoppers, and maggots.

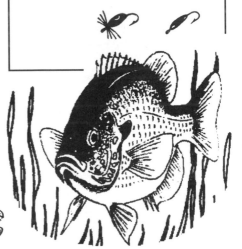

TIP 98

Spring Fishing

In the spring months, sunfish are the most active during their spawning cycle. Spawning takes place in late spring or early summer depending on the location. They will be found in the shallows, building a nest and preparing to spawn. At this time of the season, try light spinning gear or fly fishing using small wet flies, lures, or bait.

TIP 99

Summer Fishing

In the summer months, most of the larger sunfish move out of the shallows to deeper water. They are still active in the early morning or early evening hours.

Try using a spinning outfit rigged with a casting bubble with a pair of small jigs and Twister Tails tied in tandem, or try live bait or a fly-fishing outfit in the morning or evening.

TIP 100

Fall Fishing

During the fall months, sunfish remain in the deeper waters as they do in the summer months. They are still active in the early morning or early evening hours in the shallows. Try fishing for them the same way you would during the spring months. You can also try the casting-bubble method or a fly rod.

TIP 101

Winter Fishing

In the winter months, try ice fishing up north. Use a tip-up or a pole baited with wax worms or grubs. Also try jigging with ice spoons or small lures.
In the south, try fishing the same as you would in the spring or fall.

TIP 102

Where to Find Them

Perch can be found in rivers and lakes from northcentral Canada and the Great Lakes area to the Atlantic Coast and south to the Carolinas.

During the spring, look for them in the sun-warmed shallows. During the summer, they will be in deep water until the fall when they return to the shallows.

In the winter, they will again return to deep water. They feed near the bottom and can be caught with live bait.

They can be found around weed beds, docks, submerged rock piles, sunken logs, and stumps.

TIP 103
Lures

The most productive lures for perch are small jigs dressed with Twister Tails, ice spoons, small spinners, wet flies, nymph patterns, small streamers, and insect patterns.

TIP 104
Live Bait

The best live bait for perch are minnows, soft-shell crabs, worms, grubs, wax worms, crickets, grasshoppers, and maggots.

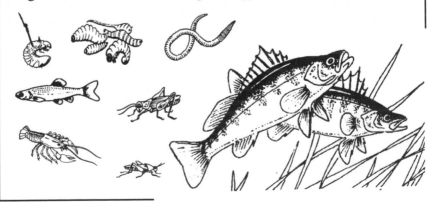

TIP 105

Spring Fishing

In the spring months, perch are the most active during their spawning cycle. Spawning takes place in the spring in the shallows. Perch are school fish, which means that if you catch one or two in a given location, there will be more around to catch. At this time of the season, try light spinning gear or fly fishing using small wet flies, lures, or live bait.

TIP 106

Summer Fishing

In the summer months, most of the larger perch move out of the shallows to deeper water. They are still active in the early morning or early evening hours.

Try using a spinning outfit rigged with jigs or spinners or a casting bubble with a pair of small jigs and Twister Tails tied in tandem. Also try live baits fished deep near the bottom.

TIP 107

Fall Fishing

During the fall months, as in the summer months, perch remain active in the deeper waters. Try fishing for them the same way you would during the summer months. You can also try the casting-bubble method.

TIP 108

Winter Fishing

In the winter months, try ice fishing up north. Use a tip-up or a pole baited with minnows, wax worms, or grubs. Also try jigging with ice spoons or small lures. In the south, try fishing the same as you would in the spring, summer, or fall.

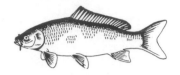

TIP 109

Where to Find Them

Carp can be found in most lakes, ponds, streams, and rivers in the United States and some parts of southern Canada. Look for them in weedy or grassy areas.

TIP 110

Equipment to Use

You can use any type of equipment (cane pole, spinning, bait casting, or even a fly-fishing outfit) to catch carp. However, make

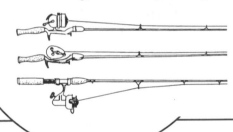

sure you have at least 100 yards of backing or 12-pound test line on your reel to handle long runs once you hook a good-size carp.

TIP 111

What Rig to Use

For the best results, try the following rig. Use the "hair rig" method to bait your hook, as shown on the following page.

Basic Rig

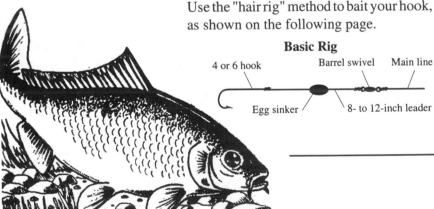

4 or 6 hook   Barrel swivel   Main line

Egg sinker   8- to 12-inch leader

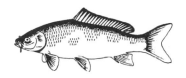

TIP 112

Hair Rigs

The "hair rig" is used by carp fishermen to mount hard baits such as maizes, peanuts, and boilies off the hook on a piece of string (hair).

By using this rig, if a carp picks up the bait and attempts to eject it, the hook remains in its mouth, giving the fisherman time to set the hook. Below are instructions on how to make your own "hair rigs" and how to bait them using a bait needle.

TIP 113

Hair-Rig Bait Needle

You can make a bait needle by taking a large sewing needle and filing a slot through one side of the needle eye. Stick the needle point into a piece of wood dowel.

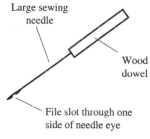

Large sewing needle

Wood dowel

File slot through one side of needle eye

Hair Rig

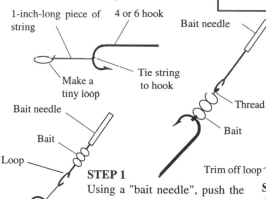

1-inch-long piece of string

4 or 6 hook

Make a tiny loop

Tie string to hook

Bait needle

Bait

Loop

STEP 1
Using a "bait needle", push the needle through two or three pieces of bait as shown. Slip the loop on the hair rig into the bait needle eye slot, and pull the string straight.

Bait needle

Thread

Bait

Trim off loop

STEP 2
Using your fingers, slide the bait over the loop onto the string and remove the needle.

STEP 3
After the bait is on the string, trim off the loop above the knot as a bait stopper or insert a grass stem to keep the bait on the string.

Sturgeons are to freshwater what sharks are to salt water. They are a prehistoric leftover that goes back a long way on the evolutionary scale. They are found throughout the world in both salt and freshwater. Heavily armored, they have a long lifespan and can grow to be 12 feet long and weigh over a thousand pounds. In the spring (April to June), they ascend rivers and streams to spawn; however, they are also known to spawn in lakes. A female sturgeon spawns every four, five, or six years upon reaching maturity at 25 years old.

TIP 114

Sturgeon Fishing

TIP 115

Sturgeon Rig

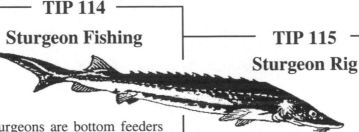

Sturgeons are bottom feeders that are mostly active after dark. They feed on crustaceans, mollusks, insect larvae, and other types of bottom organisms.

Most fishermen go after them at night from a boat or from the shore. In some states, sturgeons can be taken by spear fishing through the ice during the winter months.

Rigs used for sturgeons are similar to catfish rigs. They consist of a 7- to 9-foot salmon rod with a bait casters reel loaded with 15- to 30-pound test line. The line is attached to one of the rings on a three-way swivel with a three-foot wire leader (25- to 40-pound test) rigged with a large big-bend hook at the end of the leader and attached to another ring of the swivel.

A bell sinker on a 6- to 8-inch 8-pound test line is attached to the third ring of the swivel, and the hook is then baited with two or three night crawlers.

Wire leader

Line to rod

Three-way swivel

6- to 8-inch-long
8-pound test line

Bell sinker

Big-bend hook
baited with two or
three night crawlers

The bowfin belongs to a group of primitive bony fish that lived millions of years ago. It has a half-developed lung, allowing it to survive for hours out of water. It is found in rivers, streams, lakes, ponds, and canals throughout the Mississippi basin and southern Gulf states.

The bowfin can be found in sluggish water with weedy areas and mud bottoms. It spawns in the early spring in the shallows and remains there most of the summer and fall seasons. In the winter months, it becomes almost dormant and stays in deep water.

TIP 116

Bowfin Fishing

To catch bowfin, use a bait casting or spinning outfit with a bottom rig baited with live or cut bait.

You can also try fly fishing, using streamer flies or artificial lures with the spinning or casting gear. Once hooked, bowfin are strong fighters that provide excellent sport on light tackle.

TIP 117

Lures and Bait

The most productive lures and bait for bowfin are small spinners, spoons, and streamer patterns. The best live bait are worms, minnows, crayfish, cut bait, and frogs.

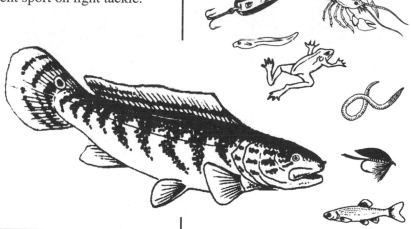

The freshwater drum can be found in lakes, rivers, and streams from the Dakotas and Great Lakes drainage system south through the Mississippi River to the Gulf of Mexico.

They are bottom feeders, and their favorite food is mollusks. They also eat insects, crayfish, and other fish species. While they can tolerate silty still waters, they prefer clean, clear water. They spawn in the spring in sandy or gravel-bottomed areas when the water temperature reaches 65 to 70 degrees.

The best time of year to fish for drum is in the late spring (May through June) and again in the fall. For the most part, they are less active during the summer months and inactive during the winter months.

TIP 118
Drum Fishing

To catch freshwater drum, use a bait casting or spinning outfit with a bottom rig baited with live or cut bait.

Experienced fishermen use a lightweight sinker just heavy enough to keep the hook on or near the bottom, or they use a presentation that keeps the bait moving slowly as they reel it in.

Many fishermen also use more than one hook per line to increase their chances of enticing the fish to bite.

TIP 119
Lures and Bait

Freshwater drum will seldom take a lure. The most productive way to catch them is with live bait, and the best bait are mollusks, worms, minnows, crayfish, cut bait, and insect larvae.

188

The gar is another living relic that belongs to a group of primitive bony fish. A number of different types are found in rivers, streams, lakes, ponds, and canals throughout the Mississippi basin and southern Gulf states.

They can be found in sluggish water with weedy areas and mud bottoms. They spawn in the early spring in the shallows and remain there most of the summer and fall seasons. In the winter months, the northern species become almost dormant and stay in deep water.

TIP 120
Gar Fishing

Most gar fishing is done in southern rivers where the alligator gar grows to 8 feet in length and weighs as much as 300 pounds.

Use heavy tackle with a 15-foot piano wire leader with a forged large hook baited with cut carp or drum. Fish in deep holes below sandbars in the channels of slow-moving streams or rivers.

Other types of gar can be taken with bow-and-arrow fishing or bottom fishing using live or cut bait.

TIP 121
Best Bait

The best live bait for the smaller gar are worms, minnows, crayfish, and cut bait.

For the alligator gar, try cut drum or carp.

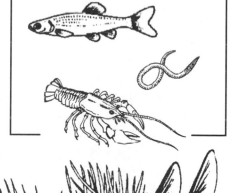

While the sucker family includes a large number of fish species, the most frequently fished for member of this family is the white sucker. Found in eastern Canada and in the northwest territories of the United States south to New Mexico, the white sucker inhabits creeks, rivers, streams, lakes, and ponds and is a bottom feeder like the carp. It spawns in the spring and fall in the shallows of creeks, streams, lakes, and ponds. Its principle foods are mollusks and crustaceans.

TIP 122

Sucker Fishing

Fishing for suckers as they migrate upstream to spawn is great sport in some areas.

They can be caught using basic spinning or casting outfits as well as fly fishing.

To catch suckers, use a bottom rig baited with live bait. They will also take a wet fly or nymph pattern when fished near the bottom.

Because of their small mouths, small hooks (about size 10) baited with worms should be used. When hooked, suckers will put up a good fight, providing a challenge for the angler.

TIP 123

Lures and Bait

The most productive flies to use when fly fishing are small wet fly and nymph patterns.

The best live bait are worms, crayfish, maggots, wax worms, and grubs.

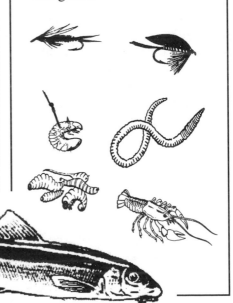

Chinook salmon grow to be the largest of all salmon, with some weighing as much as 80 pounds. They are found along the Pacific Coast of Alaska, Canada, Oregon, Washington, and California and in the Great Lakes. They spend most of their lives in salt water (with the exception of those stocked in the Great Lakes) before returning to their spawning grounds after four years to spawn and die.

TIP 124
Chinook Salmon Fishing

The chinook can be caught with a variety of fishing equipment, including spinning, bait casting, and fly-fishing gear.

Spinning or casting lures along riverbanks or bait fishing with spawn, worms, or other types of bait can be productive.

In larger rivers or in the Great Lakes region, trolling can be very effective. The most exciting method to test a fisherman's skill is with a fly-rod, wading and fly fishing in a river or stream.

TIP 125
Lures and Bait

The best lures to use are spoons, wobbling plugs, and spinners.

When fly fishing, use wet flies, streamers, and nymph patterns. The best live bait are spawn sacs, cut bait, alewives, and smelt.

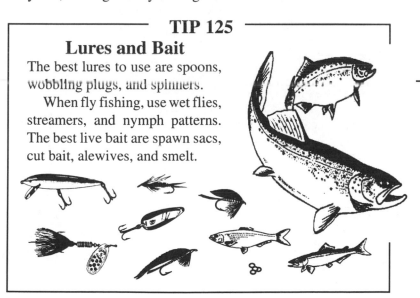

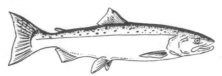

Coho salmon, which are called Atlantic salmon on the East Coast, can grow to weigh as much as 33 pounds. They are found along the Pacific Coast of Alaska, Canada, Oregon, Washington, and California, along the Atlantic Coast from northern Quebec to Connecticut, and in the Great Lakes region. Like the Chinook, they spend most of their lives in salt water (with the exception of those stocked in the Great Lakes) before returning to their spawning grounds after three years to spawn and die.

TIP 126

Coho Salmon Fishing

Coho can be caught using spinning, bait casting, and fly-fishing gear.

They are active when the water temperature is between 44 and 58 degrees, with the peak feeding temperature at 54 degrees.

Try spinning or casting lures along riverbanks or bait fishing with spawn, worms, or other types of bait. In larger rivers or in the Great Lakes region, trolling also produces good catches.

The most exciting method to test a fisherman's skill is with a fly-rod, wading and fly fishing in a river or stream.

TIP 127

Lures and Bait

The best lures for coho are spoons, wobbling plugs, and spinners. When fly fishing, use wet flies, streamers, and nymph patterns. The best live bait are spawn sacs, cut baits, alewives, and smelt.

Brown trout are not native to the United States but were introduced in 1883 from Europe. Brown trout are found throughout much of the United States, but are most prevalent in the northern section and the Great Lakes region of the country. They are known to reach a weight of 38 pounds or more and are one of the most wary members of the trout family.

Their primary foods are aquatic and terrestrial insects. Brown trout can be caught on a year-round basis but are the most active when the water temperature is between 50 and 65 degrees.

TIP 128

Brown Trout Fishing

Brown trout can be caught using spinning, bait casting, and fly-fishing gear.

Try spinning or casting lures along riverbanks or live-bait fishing.

In larger rivers or in the Great Lakes region, trolling also produces good catches. Wading and fly fishing in a river or stream are also very effective.

TIP 129

Lures and Bait

The best lures for brown trout are spoons, wobbling plugs, and spinners. When fly fishing, use wet flies, streamers, and nymph patterns for the best results. The best live bait are spawn sacs, cut baits, alewives, and smelt.

Brook trout live about four years and grow to be about 10 inches in length. A five-pounder is considered a real lunker. Brook trout are found from Ontario, Canada, east to Labrador, across much of the Rocky and Appalachian mountain areas, and in the Great Lakes region of the United States.

Brook trout have been most successfully transplanted in the northern section and the Great Lakes region of the United States. Brookies feed on aquatic and terrestrial insects and freshwater crustaceans, making them a prime target of the fly fisherman.

TIP 130
Brook Trout Fishing

For the most part, fly fishing should be the method used to catch brook trout. However, you can also use a spinning outfit for live-bait fishing or a casting bubble and fly.

You can find brook trout in cold-water lakes and streams with gravel or sandy bottoms.

They are most active in water with a temperature ranging between 48 and 64 degrees.

TIP 131
Lures and Bait

The best fly patterns to use for brookies are wet flies, dry flies, streamers, scuds, and nymphs. The best live bait are minnows, spawn sacs, insect larvae, grasshoppers or crickets, and crustaceans.

Lake trout are only native to North America and are found in deep cold lakes where the water contains a large amount of oxygen. Lake trout are found from Labrador, Canada, to Alaska and southwest to Montana and from the Great Lakes region east to northern New England.

Lake trout feed mostly on baitfish, such as shiners, chubs, smelt, or alewife. They also eat aquatic insect larvae and freshwater crustaceans. They spawn in the fall in gravel or rocky bottoms as deep as 100 feet. They are most active when the water temperature is 44 to 53 degrees, with their peak feeding temperature at 51 degrees.

TIP 132

Lake Trout Fishing

Lake trout can be taken near the surface of shallow water in the spring with live bait or lures. For the most part, deep-water trolling is the best method to use to catch lake trout; however, you can also use a spinning outfit or try fly fishing. They will hit spinners, spoons, plugs, and assorted flies. When using live bait such as alewives or smelt, fish them near the bottom.

TIP 133

Lures and Bait

The best lures and bait to use for lake trout are spinners, spoons, plugs, streamers, wet flies, and nymphs. The best live bait are minnows, shiners, alewives, and smelt.

195

Rainbow trout and steelheads are probably the best-known members of the trout family. Rainbows are the inland members, while steelheads are the sea-going ones. Rainbows live seven to eleven years and grow to an average length of 12 inches, although some get as large as 40 inches or more and weigh as much as 37 pounds.

Rainbows are found along the Pacific Coast from Alaska to Mexico, from Ontario, Canada, east to Labrador, across much of the Rocky and Appalachian mountain areas, and in the Great Lakes region of the United States. They feed on aquatic and terrestrial insects and freshwater crustaceans, making them a prime target of the fly fisherman. They are exceptional fighters on light tackle.

TIP 134

Rainbow Trout Fishing

For the most part, fly fishing should be the method used to catch rainbow trout; however, you can also use a spinning outfit for live-bait fishing or a casting bubble and fly. You can find rainbow trout in cold-water lakes and streams with gravel or sandy bottoms. They are most active in water with a temperature ranging between 50 and 65 degrees, with their peak feeding temperature at 60 degrees.

TIP 135

Lures and Bait

The best fly patterns to use for rainbows are wet flies, dry flies, streamers, scuds, and nymphs. The best live bait are worms, minnows, insect larvae, grasshoppers or crickets, and crustaceans.

Whitefish grow to be about 17 inches in length and weigh from 2 to 4 pounds. They are found in northern New England, through the Great Lakes region, and from Newfoundland west to Alaska.

Whitefish are deep-water fish that feed on aquatic insects, freshwater crustaceans, and small baitfish. Most members of the whitefish family spawn in the spring in the shallows, while some also spawn in the fall from October to December. They can be caught in deep water during the summer months, in the shallows during the spring and fall, or through the ice during the winter months.

TIP 137

Lures and Bait

The best fly-fishing patterns to use for whitefish are wet flies, dry flies, scuds, and nymph patterns. The best live bait are minnows, worms, grubs, wax worms, maggots, and crayfish.

TIP 136

Whitefish Fishing

Whitefish can be caught using spinning, bait casting, and fly-fishing gear. In addition, ice fishing for whitefish has become popular in recent years. In the spring, try fly fishing or a spinning outfit with a casting bubble. In the winter, try ice fishing in deep water with a tip-up.

When fishing for whitefish in deep water where light is limited, attach a pearl button to a small hook baited with a grub or wiggler. The button will reflect any light present, attracting the whitefish to your bait.

The sauger may lack the popularity of the walleye, but it's just as much fun to catch. Saugers grow to be about 15 inches in length and weigh from 4 to 5 pounds. A 5-pounder is considered a real lunker.

Saugers are found in Saskatchewan, Manitoba, and Ontario, Canada, in the Appalachian mountain area south to Alabama, and from the Great Lakes region west to Wyoming. Saugers prefer large river systems and move into lakes and tributary streams to spawn in the spring. They feed on aquatic and terrestrial insects, small fish, and freshwater crustaceans.

TIP 138
Sauger Fishing

Saugers can be caught by trolling, casting, still fishing, bait casting, or spinning. They will hit a variety of artificial lures, jigs, or live-bait presentations. Fish areas with sandy bottoms or just below dams or the mouths of tributaries, keeping your presentation close to the bottom.

Saugers feed both day and night, although the nighttime hours are the best for fishing.

TIP 139
Lures and Bait

The best lures for saugers are spinners, wobbly spoons, and jigs. The best live bait are minnows, worms, insect larvae, crayfish, tadpoles, and frogs.

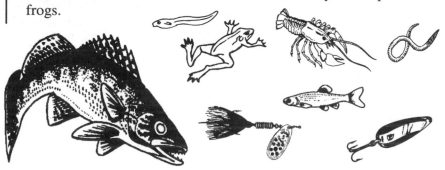

Walleye are the largest members of the perch family. They can be found in Saskatchewan, Manitoba, and Ontario, Canada, in the Appalachian Mountain area south to Alabama, and from the Great Lakes region west to Wyoming.

Deep-water fish, walleye prefer clear, large lakes with sandy or gravel bottoms. They are also found in river systems and move into lakes and tributary streams to spawn in the spring. They feed on aquatic and terrestrial insects, small fish, and freshwater crustaceans, mostly at night.

TIP 140
Night Fishing

Do the following before you go night fishing for walleye:

- Check out the area you plan to fish during daylight. Locate structure, snags, and so forth.
- Mark the spots to be fished with buoy markers during daylight.
- If trolling, plan your passes during daylight. Set the depths you plan to troll after dark.
- Organize your boat, tackle box, and equipment prior to going out.
- Take along some good lighting (flashlight, headlamp, lantern).
- Try fluorescent or lighted floats for still fishing.
- Try fluorescent lures or jigs, or add a piece of reflective tape to your favorite lures.

TIP 141
Lures and Bait

The best lures for walleye are spinners, wobbly spoons, and jigs. The best live bait are minnows, worms, insect larvae, crayfish, tadpoles, and frogs.

Smelt look like overgrown minnows that attain a length of 6 to 9 inches. However, they have been known to grow as long as 16 inches. Every spring, smelt ascend streams and rivers to spawn before returning to deeper water. Smelt can be found along the East Coast of North America from Labrador, Canada, to the Great Lakes region and south to New Jersey.

Smelt fishing during nighttime hours is an annual spring ritual in many of the Great Lakes states.

TIP 142

Smelt Fishing

Smelt can be caught during their spring runs using hook and line and live bait. The best method, however, is to use a gill net, a dip net, or a seine. The seine is pulled through the water along a beach. The dip net is attached to a boom that is lowered and raised in the water. The gill net rides up and down a trolley.

All of these nets should be placed in the path of the spawning smelt.

TIP 143

Smelting Rig

The following illustration shows the best rig to use for smelting.

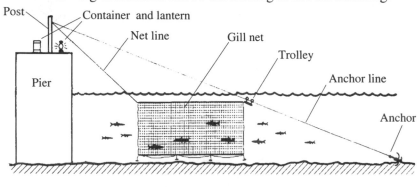

TIP LIST

TIP LIST

Chapter 6-Ice Fishing Tips *continued*   Page

Chapter 7-Fly-Fishing Tips

Chapter 10-Fishing Tips by Species